WISCONSIN CHEESE COOKBOOK

Wisconsin Cheese
COOKBOOK

....

CREAMY, CHEESY, SWEET, *and* SAVORY
RECIPES *from the* STATE'S BEST CREAMERIES

KRISTINE HANSEN

Globe
Pequot

GUILFORD, CONNECTICUT

Globe
Pequot

An imprint of The Rowman & Littlefield Publishing Group, Inc.
4501 Forbes Blvd., Ste. 200
Lanham, MD 20706
www.rowman.com

Distributed by NATIONAL BOOK NETWORK

British Library Cataloguing in Publication Information available

Library of Congress Cataloging-in-Publication Data

Names: Hansen, Kristine, author.
Title: Wisconsin cheese cookbook : creamy, cheesy, sweet, and savory recipes from the state's best creameries / Kristine Hansen.
Description: Guilford, Connecticut : Globe Pequot, [2019] | Includes index. |
Identifiers: LCCN 2018038069 (print) | LCCN 2018038755 (ebook) | ISBN 9781493037926 (e-book) | ISBN 9781493037919 (pbk. : alk. paper)
Subjects: LCSH: Cooking (Cheese) | Cheese—Wisconsin. | Creameries—Wisconsin. | LCGFT: Cookbooks.
Classification: LCC TX759.5.C48 (ebook) | LCC TX759.5.C48 H35 2019 (print) | DDC 641.6/73—dc23
LC record available at https://lccn.loc.gov/2018038069

Printed in the United States of America

Contents

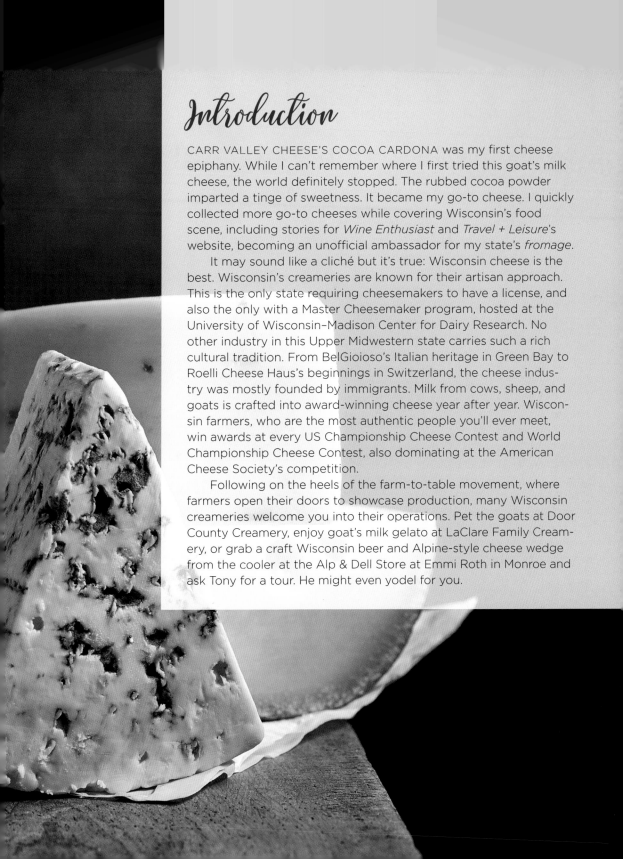

Introduction

CARR VALLEY CHEESE'S COCOA CARDONA was my first cheese epiphany. While I can't remember where I first tried this goat's milk cheese, the world definitely stopped. The rubbed cocoa powder imparted a tinge of sweetness. It became my go-to cheese. I quickly collected more go-to cheeses while covering Wisconsin's food scene, including stories for *Wine Enthusiast* and *Travel + Leisure*'s website, becoming an unofficial ambassador for my state's *fromage*.

It may sound like a cliché but it's true: Wisconsin cheese is the best. Wisconsin's creameries are known for their artisan approach. This is the only state requiring cheesemakers to have a license, and also the only with a Master Cheesemaker program, hosted at the University of Wisconsin–Madison Center for Dairy Research. No other industry in this Upper Midwestern state carries such a rich cultural tradition. From BelGioioso's Italian heritage in Green Bay to Roelli Cheese Haus's beginnings in Switzerland, the cheese industry was mostly founded by immigrants. Milk from cows, sheep, and goats is crafted into award-winning cheese year after year. Wisconsin farmers, who are the most authentic people you'll ever meet, win awards at every US Championship Cheese Contest and World Championship Cheese Contest, also dominating at the American Cheese Society's competition.

Following on the heels of the farm-to-table movement, where farmers open their doors to showcase production, many Wisconsin creameries welcome you into their operations. Pet the goats at Door County Creamery, enjoy goat's milk gelato at LaClare Family Creamery, or grab a craft Wisconsin beer and Alpine-style cheese wedge from the cooler at the Alp & Dell Store at Emmi Roth in Monroe and ask Tony for a tour. He might even yodel for you.

The numbers are astounding. Six hundred cheese varieties, types, and styles. Thousands of awards. Three billion pounds of cheese produced annually. But only around 150 creameries exist today, a sharp dive from the state's 1,500 cheese factories that existed in 1899. Wisconsin's cheesemakers are a hardworking bunch. According to the Dairy Farmers of Wisconsin, if Wisconsin were a country, it would rank fourth in world cheese production.

Ninety-six percent of Wisconsin's dairy farms are family-owned, which is the case for almost all the creameries featured in this book. In the rare case that a company or corporation does own a particular creamery, this does not change the fact that an individual or immigrant started the creamery, borrowing from a previous generation's knowledge in Europe. Partnerships, too, are common in Wisconsin's dairy industry, including Red Barn Family Farms and Organic Valley. Both source milk from small family farms and produce cheese under their labels. These groups provide marketing muscle to small farms that might be too busy juggling milking cows with making cheese to support administrative tasks.

Cow's Milk Cheese

By far, cow's milk makes up the bulk of Wisconsin's cheese production. There's a huge range in flavor and texture that can arise from this milk source, which is part of what makes it a popular choice for cheesemakers. And if you've spent any time in the Dairy State, you know that it's not uncommon to see towering faux Holstein cows at truck stops off the interstate or at state and county fairs each summer, and living and breathing cows along rural roads. The cows that source milk to the Wisconsin cheese industry are Holstein (these are the black-and-white cows) and Jersey (light brown and white). In some cases, hybrid breeds exist, with the sole purpose of producing the best milk possible. Jersey cows are native to the Channel Islands off the coast of France. Many Wisconsin dairy farms never have to buy cows—instead, they breed from their own, which is a testament to the quality of care.

Cheesemakers in Wisconsin say that what makes their cheese so tasty is the quality of the cows' milk. This philosophy is not that different from winemakers who search high and low for the best wine grapes. It all goes back to the soil and, to borrow a French term, *terroir*. What grasses and other naturally occurring feed the cows eat—or where the grape vines grow—depends on the soil's sediment: Is it loamy, rocky, with limestone, or sandy? A few Wisconsin cheesemakers, in fact, release special cheeses on a seasonal basis that are 100 percent based on the animals' diet. Uplands Cheese, a farmstead in Dodgeville, retails its Pleasant Ridge Reserve (crafted with grass-fed milk during the summer) and Rush Creek Reserve (the fall season's milk changes based on the cows' hay diet) at nearly $30 a pound, and you can find it at high-end cheese shops in California and New York City. It's worth every penny. And in true Wisconsin homegrown fashion, a poster illustration is released with each cheese vintage, designed by cheesemaker Andy Hatch's wife, Caitlin.

Goat's Milk Cheese

A rising number of cheesemakers in Wisconsin are using goat's milk cheese, including LaClare Family Creamery in Malone, which began as a goat farm during the 1970s and, now on its second generation, has evolved into a creamery. Cheesemaker Katie Fuhrmann, one of the five children, got the bright idea one day to start making cheese from their goats' milk. That inspiration paid off big time: She won the "Best of Show" award for Evalon, an aged goat cheese, at the 2011 US Championship Cheese Contest.

You might think that goat cheese—marked by its bright, acidic flavor and tangy accents—is only sold as a fresh log (chèvre), but that's actually not true. Goat's milk cheese can also be aged into hard, block-style wedges, which is most of what LaClare sells.

Other goat's milk cheese producers include Door County Creamery in idyllic Door County, wedged between Lake Michigan and Green Bay. Justin and Rachael Johnson take the milk from goats on his family's farm and use it to craft cheeses sold in their Sister Bay retail store. Production from this farmstead remains small, but the creamery is still young.

Mixed-milk varieties provide cheesemakers even more flexibility, which is what Sid Cook at Carr Valley Cheese advocates. For example, his Mobay, a take on the French cheese style of Morbier, took second place in its category in the 2017 US Championship Cheese Contest and third place in the 2014 World Championship Cheese Contest.

Sheep's Milk Cheese

Only a handful of Wisconsin's artisan cheeses are made from sheep's milk, which brings a higher fat content to the cheese. This translates to a super buttery and rich flavor. Nordic Creamery and Hidden Springs Creamery—both in the Driftless Region town of Westby—are two of those. But don't be fooled by their small size. Nordic Creamery's cheeses and butters are served at high-end hotels and restaurants in Chicago, including the Four Seasons Hotel Chicago, and each Saturday during the warmer months they are sold at Green City Market, which is where all the city's chefs shop.

Cheese Pairings

The beauty of pairing cheese with beverages—wine, beer, and spirits, including cocktails—is that, no matter what you do, the taste of either won't suffer. But if you keep these rules in mind, the flavor of your favorite cheese will only be accentuated.

Like with Like

What are some signature notes in the cheese? If it's rubbed in a spice, look for a drink that captures some of that same heat, such as a Cabernet Sauvignon with a spicy finish or a cocktail featuring chipotle or jalapeño. Should the cheese feature fruity notes, search out a fruit-forward wine like Beaujolais from France or a California Zinfandel. For a true Wisconsin pairing, sip New Glarus Brewing Company's Wisconsin Belgian Red with Sartori's BellaVitano (soaked with Raspberry Tart ale). Similarities in each will make the flavor notes sing, but not shout for attention.

Texture

A rich, creamy goat cheese might not be the best match for a dry Spanish red. Let's unpack the reasons why. Pairings should not fight for attention. Instead, they should be harmonious, on the same level in terms of intensity and flavor, not to mention texture. Is the cheese creamy or hard? Does the beverage sit on your palate long after you've swallowed or does it slip away seamlessly? Back to that goat cheese example: Try sipping a chalky Chablis wine from France or a hoppy Wisconsin beer. If you truly want to drink a dry Spanish red, turn to an aged cheddar. Sparkling wines often taste best with creamy cheeses. Try Crave Brothers Mascarpone with Sparkler, a sparkling wine produced by Parallel 44 Vineyard and Winery in Kewaunee. This wine won "Best in Show" at the first annual Wine is Wisconsin competition at the University of Wisconsin–Madison in 2017.

Regional

Truly stuck on what to drink with a particular cheese? Pick up a beverage produced in the same county as that cheese. This is what Europe has been practicing for centuries—for example, an English cheddar with a strong ale or a provolone with Chianti. The idea is that these products come from the same climate, which includes *terroir*, and are already linked in flavor.

In Wisconsin you can take this to the extreme. Door County Creamery's goat cheeses are made within a short bicycle ride of many wineries. Try a Marquette Forte dessert-style wine from Harbor Ridge Winery in Egg Harbor, seventeen miles south, with one of Door County Creamery's flavored chèvre, like cherries or truffles, or even the French Feta.

Wollersheim's Domaine Du Sac, made from grapes (90 percent Marechal Foch and 10 percent Millot) grown on vines overlooking the Wisconsin River, pairs well with many cheeses made in that region, such as those from Carr Valley Cheese, Hook's Cheese, and Cedar Grove, which all feature milk sourced locally.

Southwest Wisconsin

GREEN COUNTY AND THE DRIFTLESS REGION are home to the highest concentration of award-winning cheese in America. Grassy peaks and carved valleys, unchanged during the ice age's glacial shifts, prove to be a nice resting place for cows, sheep, and goats, whose milk is woven into all this amazing cheese. Young organic farmers work alongside multi-generational Amish families, both passionate about living off the land.

What makes the cheese so delicious? It's the milk. Another factor is the relationships between cheesemakers and dairy farmers. Some date back four generations, united by a bond to keep their businesses small and family-owned. Many learned to make cheese from Swiss relatives who moved here as young immigrants chasing an American dream. And yet a younger generation is emerging, people like Andy Hatch who, in his thirties, serves as cheese-maker and co-owner with his wife and another couple of Uplands Cheese, making just two cheeses each year that are sold in high-end cheese shops around the country.

Reflecting that Swiss heritage most deeply is the Green County town of Monroe, home to Emmi Roth, one of the state's largest creameries. Visitors can enjoy a pot of fondue with a glass of Wisconsin wine and witness cheese being made. Several micro creameries like Roelli Cheese Haus put out fine cheeses that are true Alpine style, stemming from ancestors who learned to do the same task in the Swiss Alps and, fortunately, brought that skill to Wisconsin. Many Driftless Region cheesemakers—like Tony Hook of Hook's Cheese and Willi Lehner of Bleu Mont Dairy—flock to the country's largest producer-only farmers' market, hosted on Madison's Capitol Square every Saturday morning. Rubbing elbows with chicken farmers, Amish bakers, and growers of specialty vegetable crops is a fitting tribute to this agricultural belt, where boutique approaches to doing business are respected and revered.

Bleu Mont Dairy

WILLI LEHNER'S PARENTS EMIGRATED FROM SWITZERLAND to Wisconsin during the 1950s. Drawing upon expertise gained back in Switzerland, his dad landed a job at a Mount Horeb creamery. Lehner watched his dad make Swiss, Muenster, and cheddar cheese. "I was in charge of waxing," he quips. "I remember how good the flavor was in those cheeses."

"As a kid, Dad taught me about the quality of milk (cows feeding on grass, not grain), but it wasn't until I went to Switzerland and helped a friend make cheese in an alpine pasture and saw what the cows ate that I got it," says Lehner. He noticed that what animals eat influences the final product. What makes Wisconsin milk so well suited for cheese? "A lot of it has to do with the calcium in the soil," he says.

Lehner experienced an epiphany tasting clothbound cheddar from Great Britain as an adult. "I tasted it and went 'Oh my god, this is sensational cheese,'" says Lehner. Several seasons spent in Switzerland's Bernese Alps taught him how to make cheese using a copper kettle over an open flame. Through a grant from the University of Wisconsin–Madison's Center for Dairy Research, he studied cheddar production in Great Britain.

Bleu Mont Dairy's production is small: four batches of 320 wheels twice a year (spring and fall), followed by twelve to eighteen months of aging in dome-like caves just behind Lehner's house, built into the grassy hillside. "I don't make cheese in the winter. Winter's for skiing," says Lehner, who spends much of each winter in Jackson Hole, Wyoming. Distribution isn't limited to Wisconsin: Murray's Cheese in New York City carries Bleu Mont Dairy's cheese.

Willi's college-age daughter lives in Zurich, Switzerland, studying sustainability in agricultural systems and policy at ETH. "Whenever we go to Switzerland, he comes home with a couple of wheels (of cheese)," says his partner, Kitas McKnight. "He eats more cheese than anyone else I've met." Sure enough, two wedges are out on the kitchen counter on a drizzly day in May. Lehner slices off a hunk of his Alpine Renegade and considers its flavor profile. Like any man who knows his cheese, he responds that it needs "another three to four months."

"The Bandaged Cheddar grated on top of asparagus is so good. Those flavors just work," says Kitas McKnight.

"Whenever I make quiches, I put a layer (of the cheese) on the bottom and on the top."

Kale Ddeokbokki

4 cups chicken stock or vegetable stock

1 onion, sliced

1 tablespoon minced garlic

1 tablespoon minced ginger

1 package rice logs, cut into thirds and soaked in cold water for at least 1 hour or overnight

1 bunch kale

6-8 perilla leaves (shiso leaves)

2 links Lap Cheong (Chinese sausage), cut into bite-size pieces

4 hard-boiled eggs, chopped

2 tablespoons (or to taste) fish sauce

1 tablespoon (or to taste) sugar

GARNISH:

Bleu Mont Dairy Bandaged Cheddar, shredded

Korean chili flakes

Sesame seeds

Scallions

In a stockpot, heat stock to a boil. Add onion, garlic, ginger, and rice logs. Simmer, reducing by half, until thickened and rice logs are tender.

Boil kale until tender in salted water, then shock in ice water. Blend cooked kale with perilla leaves and a bit of ice water. Cook sausage on stovetop, turning until browned and crisp, about 3 minutes. Add kale puree and chopped eggs to cooked rice logs and bite-size sausage pieces, then fish sauce and sugar, adjusting for taste.

Garnish with shredded cheese, chili flakes, sesame seeds, and sliced scallions. Serve immediately.

Recipe by Tory Miller, chef/owner Sujeo Restaurant in Madison

SERVES 4

The Charmant Hotel

101 State St
La Crosse, WI
(608) 519-8800
thecharmanthotel.com

On a sunny evening in early June, I settled into a table at the sixty-seven-room Charmant Hotel's ground-floor restaurant. The Mississippi River was on my right, viewable through floor-to-ceiling windows, the industrial-era decor of the sun-dappled massive dining space to my left.

The process of taking my order went more like a conversation than me reading off the dinner menu. That's because adjustments are made based on what arrived in the kitchen from local farmers that morning. Case in point: the cheese plate. Its three to five selections were not entirely known to me until it was set in front of me. That's the beauty of dining local: You are at the whim of the region's soil. Some years the tomato harvest might be late or the ramps come in earlier than ever before. A good chef, just like executive chef Spencer Schaller at the Charmant Hotel, knows how to work with flux.

In the heart of the Driftless Region, one of America's most concentrated organic-farm belts, and home to the Organic Valley cooperative, the Charmant Hotel's culinary staff considers this to be a welcome challenge. It's also a fitting second chapter to this brick building, which opened in 1898 as a candy factory, staying in operation for the next thirty-five years. Guests are immediately reminded of this heritage upon check-in when they are handed two chocolates. The hotel opened its doors in late 2015.

Other cheese dishes on the menu include Old Country Creamery cheese curds with house ranch dressing and a burger topped with Hook's Colby. A starter of goat cheese, too, is paired with local Amish honey.

French Onion Soup

2 cups chopped onions

⅔ cup brandy

4 quarts (16 cups) beef or chicken stock

2 bay leaves

10 thyme sprigs

3 tablespoons Worcestershire sauce

Salt and pepper, to taste

Gruyère, to top

Sauté onions in frying pan until caramelized, then deglaze with brandy.

Add stock, bay leaves, thyme, and Worcestershire sauce and simmer for 10 minutes, seasoning with salt and pepper to taste.

Spoon in baking dish and top with Gruyère. Bake at 400°F until top is golden brown and cheese has melted, becoming bubbly and slightly toasted, about 7 to 10 minutes.

Recipe by the Charmant Hotel

SERVES 24

Carr Valley Cheese

MASTER CHEESEMAKER SID COOK is a legend when it comes to Wisconsin cheese. He's won more awards than any other cheesemaker in the world—somewhere around seven hundred. In fact, he won twelve at the first competition he entered, in 2002 at the American Cheese Society's competition in Washington, DC.

Crafting around one hundred varieties of cheese—but specializing in cheddars and fontina, sourcing cow's, sheep's, and goat's milk, and doing a mix of smoking and aging—Cook is inspired by his great-grandfather's brother's legacy. In 1883 Ed Lepley began making cheese at a factory in nearby Viola at the age of thirteen. Cook got his cheese-maker license at sixteen. His grandparents were also cheesemakers.

Carr Valley Cheese, which Sid purchased in 1986, continues to be family-run. His son works in the Mauston plant, his stepdaughter (Andrea Christoff) oversees social media, and his son-in-law (Dave Christoff) works in sales.

Two years ago, Carr Valley Cheese branched out into butter. Eight stores are open in Mazomanie, Middleton, Sauk City, Mauston, Fennimore, La Valle, and Wisconsin Dells. A blue-cheese factory in Linden joined the company in 2011. Exports of Carr Valley Cheese cross oceans to places such as Japan, Taiwan, Hong Kong, France, Germany, Australia, and Nicaragua. When Cook skis in Colorado—as he often does—he sometimes even spots his own products. "I was skiing at Vail and at a restaurant and what do they have there? Gorgonzola from Carr Valley."

Cook believes strongly in getting to know his customers—not just selling through distributors. This is why Carr Valley Cheese has so many stores. "We like to sell to our consumer because it drives our brand nationally," he says.

Cheese is never not in abundance at the Cook household. "We always have twelve to fourteen different cheeses in the fridge," he says. "I really like the blue cheeses. With the Billy Blue (smoked blue goat cheese) I'll make a cream sauce, for pasta al dente." Another favorite snack? That same sauce spread on toast with honey drizzled on top. Cook also likes putting blue cheese in a salad of greens and sliced pears. Blue cheese is also used in a layered potato dish. "We always have that on Christmas dinner, with a prime rib," he says. But for everyday consumption, it's his smoked pepper jack cheese he likes. "This is a great beer-drinking cheese."

Growing up, Cook's relatives always put out a hearty spread for meals. "There was always cheese. Lunch was 'whenever you stopped by,'" says Cook, who recalls berries with cream, pies, and sandwich fixings like pickles, ham, jelly, honey, bread, and—of course—cheese.

Supreme Macaroni and Cheese with Carr Valley Fontina and 3-Year Cheddar

1 (16-ounce) package elbow macaroni

½ cup (1 stick) butter

½ cup all-purpose flour

2 cups half-and-half

2 cups milk

1 teaspoon salt

1 teaspoon dry mustard

2 cups shredded **Carr Valley Fontina**

3 cups shredded **Carr Valley 3 Year Aged Cheddar,** divided

3 teaspoons fresh chives, optional

1 cup cornflake crumbs tossed with 1 tablespoon melted butter

Preheat oven to 375°F. Lightly grease a large baking/casserole dish.

Cook macaroni according to package directions.

In a saucepan, melt butter over medium heat and stir in flour until smooth. Add half-and-half, milk, and salt, stirring with a whisk until thickened. Add mustard, then gradually add fontina, 2 cups cheddar (reserving 1 cup for topping), and chives, stirring until cheese has melted.

Combine sauce and macaroni, then transfer to baking dish and layer remaining cheddar over top. Sprinkle with buttered cornflake crumbs and bake for 20 minutes.

SERVES 6

Fried Potato Chips with Spicy Blue Cheese Sauce

POTATO CHIPS:

2 pounds unpeeled potatoes
(7–8 medium)

Oil for frying

Salt

BLUE CHEESE SAUCE:

2 tablespoons unsalted butter

2 tablespoons all-purpose flour

2½ cups whole milk, room
temperature

½ teaspoon cayenne pepper

¾ pound crumbled **Carr Valley
Glacier Wildfire Blue**

FOR POTATO CHIPS:

Wash and peel potatoes. Slice very thin.

Place slices in a bowl of salted ice water immediately after cutting, and let stand for at least 30 minutes.

Completely dry potato slices before frying in hot oil (at 390°F) until light golden brown. Drain on paper towels and salt lightly.

FOR BLUE CHEESE SAUCE:

Melt butter in a saucepan, stirring in flour, and cook for 1 minute. Slowly whisk in milk, and continue whisking until thickened.

Remove from heat and stir in cayenne pepper and Glacier Wildfire Blue cheese. If sauce is too thick, thin with extra milk.

SERVES 8

Apple Pie with Sharp Cheddar Crust

2¼ cups all-purpose flour

1 teaspoon sugar

1 teaspoon salt

1 cup (2 sticks) unsalted butter, cold, cut into pieces

1 cup shredded **Carr Valley 4 Year Aged Cheddar,** plus additional for topping

36 ounces prepared or homemade apple-pie filling

1 egg

Splash of cold water or milk

FOR CHEDDAR PIE CRUST:

Combine flour, sugar, and salt in a bowl. Add butter pieces and, with a pastry blender, cut butter into flour until crumbly. Add cheese.

Add 4 tablespoons cold water. Divide dough in half and let rest for 30–45 minutes.

FOR PIE:

Preheat oven to 400°F.

Roll out half of dough on a lightly floured surface and place in a greased 9-inch pie dish. Add apple-pie filling.

Roll out other half of dough and place on top of pie, sealing edges and trimming excess dough.

Brush pie with egg wash (egg beaten with cold water or milk) and cut air slits in the center.

Bake for 60 minutes on a baking sheet or until crust is golden brown.

Remove from oven and top with additional cheddar, then cool to room temperature.

SERVES 8

Sid's 101-year-old mother, Merna, serves this pie often. "I like that big, bold fruity acid flavor," says Sid.

Roasted Root Vegetables with Carr Valley Snow White Goat Cheddar

1 large sweet potato, peeled and cut into wedges

1 large turnip, peeled and cut into 1-inch pieces

2 medium beets, peeled and cut into wedges

3 medium carrots, peeled and cut into 1-inch pieces

¼ cup extra-virgin olive oil

Salt and pepper, to taste

8 ounces **Carr Valley Snow White Goat Cheddar,** rind removed

Preheat oven to 400°F.

Combine vegetables, olive oil, salt, and pepper in a large bowl. Transfer vegetables to a baking sheet and bake for 40 minutes or until soft enough to pierce with a fork.

Using a vegetable peeler, shave goat cheddar into thin strips.

Remove vegetables from oven and sprinkle with cheese while still warm.

Serve warm.

SERVES 8

"Our Snow White Goat Cheddar is incredible shaved on any warm roasted root vegetable," says Andrea Christoff.

Dane County Farmers' Market
Capitol Square

Madison

Saturday 6:15 a.m. to 1:45 p.m.

Never is Madison more alive than on a Saturday morning between April and November on Capitol Square. No, there is not a protest or University of Wisconsin Badgers sporting event—this is the country's largest producer-only farmers' market.

Pedestrian traffic, to the tune of twenty thousand visitors each weekend, is so thick that you must walk in one direction around the square, and you will inevitably brush elbows with others. Amish farmers sell scones, breads, and muffins next to thirty-something farming couples who gave it all up to live off the land, and Hmong farmers participate in the market, too. Since 1972 this market has been in full swing and always on the square. Former mayor Bill Dyke had been inspired by Europe's open markets and sought to bring a similar concept to Madison. Only the concept took a while to land with farmers: The first market drew only five vendors but quickly grew to dozens of vendors each week. Two years later the number of farmers participating had evolved to more than 100. There is now a two- to three-year waiting list for farmers to participate.

Today you should definitely pick up Hot & Spicy Cheese Bread from Stella's Bakery. This bakery, currently owned by Brian and Julie Winzenried, has been in business since 1988 and is an institution in Madison.

Creameries like Bleu Mont Dairy, Farmer Johns' Cheese, Forgotten Valley Cheese, Hook's Cheese, Capri Cheese, Brunkow Cheese, Crème de la Coulee, McCluskey Brothers, LaClare Family Creamery, and Murphy Farms offer samples and sell wedges of their cheese. It's important to these cheesemakers that they put a face to their product, establishing relationships with customers over morning coffee each weekend. For cheese lovers, it's a dream come true to be able to try, with your little toothpick, a dozen cheese varieties at one stand alone. Prices tend to be competitive, too, with local retailers, so definitely don't be shy about stocking up.

Local chefs choose to shop at the farmers' market, keeping the farm-to-table movement alive, whether that's cheese or greens, or even meats, all made locally by boutique food producers.

Visiting Madison during the week? Dane County Farmers' Market also runs a market Wednesday between 8:30 a.m. and 1:45 p.m. (between mid-April and mid-November) in the 200 block of Martin Luther King, Jr. Boulevard, a block off Capitol Square. During the other months, the market moves to indoor locations, keeping its year-round status.

Cedar Grove Cheese

BY RUNNING ONE OF THE AREA'S first cheese factories—in business since 1878—Bob Wills is a conscientious steward of Wisconsin's culinary history.

"At one time there were 2,600 cheese factories in the state," says Wills. "There were 21 within seven miles of here." Fewer creameries resulted in a shift from commodity to artisan, specialty cheeses. "We went from being a state that made Colby and cheddar—and Swiss in the southern part of the state—to realizing there were a lot of opportunities and we could compete nationally. There's been a significant rebirth of the industry here."

Today rolling green hills in Sauk County part to reveal a long road leading to Cedar Grove Cheese, where the flagship cheese is cheese curds, nearly twenty-six thousand pounds churned out per week. Milk is sourced from local farms, including one in continuous operation for around a century. A retail store sells Cedar Grove cheese. Also on the property is one of the state's most successful eco-agriculture projects, a "living machine" that's a natural water treatment system augmented with tropical plants. It's fitting as Wills once worked for environmental pioneer and Earth Day founder Gaylord Nelson. "It is a unique and innovative way to not only clean the waste water but also to make the importance of clean water more visible for our employees and visitors," says Wills. "The water reaches a quality that enables us to return it to the groundwater or the local creek."

Wills bought his in-laws' cheese factory in 1989, after receiving a law degree and doctorate in economics from the University of Wisconsin–Madison and working in Chicago and Washington, DC. "I wanted to do something completely different," he says. "I decided I wanted to make something." He's one of the state's Master Cheesemakers, too. Much like Wills's urban cousin—Clock Shadow Creamery in Milwaukee—he leases the factory for area cheesemakers, including Landmark Creamery and Bleu Mont Dairy, who lack their own equipment to make cheese. Wills's son Bo manages operations at Clock Shadow Creamery while son Owen chips in with sales from time to time.

Standard Wisconsin Poutine

1 medium onion, thinly sliced

1 tablespoon brown sugar

2 tablespoons butter

1 tablespoon all-purpose flour

6 ounces dark malt beer

½ cup beef stock

3 cups crispy potato tots or french fries

1 cup **Cedar Grove cheddar cheese curds**

Cook onion and brown sugar in butter until onion is translucent and begins to caramelize. Slowly stir in flour and dark malt beer. Simmer for 5 minutes. Add beef stock and reduce for 7 minutes.

Cook crispy potato tots or french fries according to package instructions.

Add curds to potatoes while still hot. Pour gravy over curds and tots and serve immediately.

SERVES 2

Wisconsin Vegetarian Poutine

Olive oil

4 sprigs fresh rosemary, minced

Garlic, minced

1 large rutabaga, peeled and diced

1 cup **Cedar Grove cheddar cheese curds**

½ cup sweet spring peas

GRAVY:

1 medium onion, thinly sliced

2 tablespoons butter

1 tablespoon brown sugar or maple syrup

1 tablespoon all-purpose flour

1½ cups vegetable broth

1 tablespoon Sriracha

Preheat oven to 400°F.

Coat a roasting pan with olive oil and add rosemary, garlic, and rutabaga. Bake for 1 hour, turning after 30 minutes.

FOR GRAVY:

Cook onion in butter until translucent and about to caramelize. Add brown sugar or maple syrup, then stir in flour. Add vegetable broth and Sriracha sauce and reduce for 10 minutes.

While still hot, cover rutabaga with 1 cup curds. Pour gravy on top.

Add peas just before serving.

SERVES 2

Crave Brothers Farmstead Cheese

CRAVE BROTHERS' HOLSTEIN COWS are clustered by grade, as if cycling through elementary school on up to high-school graduation.

George Crave runs the creamery—which crafts about fifteen thousand pounds of cheese daily—and farmstead. His wife, Debbie, handles marketing and also dips into her Italian American heritage to create recipes using their mascarpone and mozzarella. Crave Brothers also produces cheddar curds; Oaxaca, a Hispanic melting cheese; and Farmer's Rope, a braided rope cheese. Its marinated mozzarella took first place in the 2018 World Championship Cheese Contest, and its fresh mozzarella third. Crave Brothers is one of only three mascarpone makers in Wisconsin. Four years ago the company introduced a Wisconsin classic to its product line—cheese curds. All in all, Crave Brothers has won 112 awards, including for its fresh mozzarella, mascarpone, string cheese, and cheddar cheese curds.

In 1978 George and his brother Charlie rented a farm in Mount Horeb with fifty-five cows. Now they milk 1,900 cows on two sites: 1,100 at their farm and 800 on a neighboring property. For George it's a natural succession from his childhood growing up on a dairy farm, then attending the University of Wisconsin Madison's Farm & Industry Short Course, and learning to make cheese at the UW–Madison Center for Dairy Research. What draws visitors to Crave Brothers isn't just the cheese, but also a methane-gas digester system that transforms farm waste into fuel through two 750-gallon tanks. This is an eco-friendly alternative to burning diesel gas and means the farm is carbon-negative, relying solely on green power. "We're producing fuel every day to power this generator," says George, ticking off all the resources their cows now provide: milk, meat, and manure.

Several local restaurants turn to Crave Brothers for cheese, including The Bartolotta Restaurants in the Milwaukee area (fresh mozzarella at its wine events) and Hartwig's in Waterloo (cheese curds in lobster bisque).

Poised to take over the creamery as the next generation are George and Debbie's twenty-nine-year-old son Patrick (he works with the cows) and their two nephews. Their niece-in-law, Beth, works in customer service. And another son, Brian, is in production. Daughter Roseanne handles social media and some marketing activities. Diesel, Debbie and George's black lab, greets most visitors in the parking lot.

Crave Brothers Farmstead Classics Lemon Mascarpone Tarts

1 tube refrigerated sugar-cookie dough

1 jar lemon curd

1 pound **Crave Brothers Farmstead Classics Mascarpone,** room temperature

1 pint fresh raspberries

Preheat oven to 350°F.

Slice cookie dough into ¼- to ½-inch-thick discs. Slice each disc in half. Press pieces into greased mini-muffin tins.

Bake for 8–10 minutes or until golden. Cool completely.

Meanwhile, heat lemon curd in a microwaveable dish until spreadable. Whisk with mascarpone until light and airy. Fill each cookie with lemon-mascarpone filling. Top with raspberries.

Recipe by Beth Crave

MAKES 36 MINI TARTS

Crave Brothers Fresh Mozzarella Burger

6 burgers, cooked

12 Crave Brothers Fresh Mozzarella Medallions

1 cup marinara sauce

6 hamburger buns

MARINARA SAUCE:

1 medium yellow onion, chopped

1-2 tablespoons olive oil

1½ teaspoons minced garlic

½ cup red wine

1 (28-ounce) can crushed tomatoes

1 teaspoon dried oregano

1 teaspoon dried basil

½ teaspoon sugar

½ teaspoon salt

½ teaspoon black pepper

"It's a great take on burger season, to use fresh mozzarella," says Debbie Crave.

Sauté onions in olive oil over medium heat for 5–10 minutes. Add garlic and cook for 1 minute before adding wine at high heat. Scrape up brown bits until liquid evaporates, about 3 minutes. Stir in tomatoes, oregano, basil, sugar, salt, and black pepper. Cover and simmer on low for 15 minutes, stirring occasionally.

Top each burger with a generous amount of sauce, then place two mozzarella medallions on top.

Serve with buns.

SERVES 6

Crave Brothers Farmstead Classics Marinated Herbed Tomato Salad

6 ripe tomatoes, cut in wedges

3 sweet peppers (combination green, red, and yellow), sliced

1 sweet Spanish onion (white or red), sliced

1 cup pitted black olives, drained

2 (8-ounce) containers **Crave Brothers Farmstead Classics Fresh Mozzarella Cheese Ciliegine**

DRESSING:

⅔ cup vegetable oil

¼ cup red wine vinegar

¼ cup snipped fresh parsley or cilantro

¼ cup snipped green onions with tops

1 teaspoon salt

¼ teaspoon black pepper

1 teaspoon sugar

½ teaspoon dried basil (or 1 tablespoon fresh basil)

½ teaspoon dried marjoram

Slice vegetables into a bowl, then add olives and cheese.

Combine dressing ingredients in a screw-top jar and shake well. Pour dressing over vegetables. Cover and refrigerate for 3–4 hours before serving.

Recipe by Janet Crave

SERVES 6—8

Crave Brothers Farmstead Classics Chocolate Mascarpone Pie

CRUMB CRUST:

1 cup chocolate-wafer cookie crumbs

3 tablespoons sugar

4 tablespoons butter, melted, plus more for pan

FILLING:

16 ounces **Crave Brothers Farmstead Classics Mascarpone,** room temperature

6 ounces semi-sweet chocolate, melted

2 tablespoons Kahlua or Amaretto

FOR CRUMB CRUST:

Preheat oven to 325°F. Butter a 9-inch pie pan.

In a bowl, combine cookie crumbs, sugar, and melted butter, then press evenly into pan. Bake for 6 minutes. Set aside to cool.

FOR FILLING:

Stir mascarpone and chocolate in a large bowl until blended and no white streaks remain. Stir in Kahlua or Amaretto. Immediately spread filling in cooled crust. Cover and refrigerate for 1 hour.

Serve with whipped cream.

Recipe by Debbie Crave

SERVES 8

Crave Brothers Farmstead Cheese Creamy Mascarpone Mushroom Soup

1 bunch green onions, chopped (use some of the green part)

5 tablespoons butter

2 pounds assorted wild mushrooms (such as shiitake, portobello, crimini, white button), sliced

5 cups chicken broth

¾ cup port

¼ teaspoon dried thyme

1½ cups heavy cream

2 tablespoons lemon juice

⅛ teaspoon black pepper

8 ounces **Crave Brothers Farmstead Classics Mascarpone**

Sauté onions in butter in a 5-quart saucepan for 5 minutes until soft. Add mushrooms and cook about 8 minutes more or until tender. Add broth, port, and thyme. Heat to boiling. Reduce heat and simmer for 20 minutes to blend flavors.

Puree in batches using a blender. Pour puree into a large bowl. Repeat with remaining mixture, leaving 1 to 2 cups unpureed (with intact whole mushroom slices for garnish and appearance at serving). Return puree to saucepan. Add cream, lemon juice, black pepper, and mascarpone. Heat soup over low heat just until heated through.

Serve with crusty bread or breadsticks.

Recipe by Debbie Crave

SERVES 8

Crave Brothers Farmstead Classics
Fresh Mozzarella, Strawberries, and Mint Salad

½ cup extra-virgin olive oil

¼ cup fresh mint leaves

½ pint strawberries, cleaned and sliced

3 tablespoons sugar

1 (8-ounce) container **Crave Brothers Farmstead Classics Fresh Mozzarella Ovoline,** sliced ¼ inch thick

2 teaspoons balsamic vinegar, divided

Process olive oil and mint in a blender until smooth.

In a small bowl, combine strawberries and sugar and set aside.

Top mozzarella slices with strawberries and drizzle 1½ tablespoons mint mixture and ½ teaspoon balsamic vinegar over each plate. Serve immediately.

SERVES 4

Crave Brothers Mascarpone, Fig, Sweet Onion, and Candied Bacon Pizza

¼ cup brown sugar

¼ teaspoon cayenne pepper

5 strips thick-sliced bacon

14 figs, quartered

1 cup dry red wine

2 teaspoons minced fresh basil

2 large sweet onions, thinly sliced

2 tablespoons butter

1 (14-ounce ball) frozen pizza dough, thawed

1 tablespoon olive oil

1 (8-ounce) **Crave Brothers Farmstead Classics Mascarpone**

Preheat oven to 400°F. Spray pizza pan and oven-safe cooling rack with nonstick cooking spray. Line a baking sheet with aluminum foil.

In a small, shallow bowl, combine brown sugar and cayenne pepper, then dredge bacon in mixture. Bake bacon on baking sheet for 15–18 minutes until crisp and caramelized. Remove from oven and cool. Crumble bacon and set aside.

In a medium saucepan, bring figs, wine, and basil to a boil. Reduce heat and simmer for 18 minutes, until wine becomes syrupy.

Sauté onions in butter over low to medium heat for 12 minutes or until tender and caramelized.

Spread pizza dough into pizza pan and brush edges with olive oil. Spoon onions on top, then spoon fig and wine mixture evenly over onions. Top with dollops of mascarpone.

Bake on center rack for 15 minutes.

Sprinkle candied bacon on pizza and bake for another 3 minutes. Slice and serve immediately.

Recipe by Nadine Mesch

SERVES 6–8

Deja Food Group
Estrellon, L'Etoile, Graze, and Sujeo
Madison

Practically neck and neck with Alice Waters' Chez Panisse (open in Berkeley, California, since 1971) for the title of the country's first true farm-to-table restaurant, L'Etoile's chef-owner Tory Miller carries on the torch for Odessa Piper's inspiration back in the 1970s.

As founder in 1976 of this fancy restaurant on Capitol Square in Madison, Piper culled the Saturday farmers' market on the square—literally across the street—for delectable finds to put on the menu. At the time, because most chefs relied upon food-service distributors, the concept was both fascinating and foreign.

In 2005, when Piper retired, she handed the torch over to Racine, Wisconsin, native Tory Miller and his sister, Traci Miller. Since then the duo has not only kept L'Etoile in the comfortable spot of offering one of the state's best fine-dining menus featuring Wisconsin farms, but also weaves Wisconsin cheesemakers' creations into five-star dishes that are part of the seven-course nightly chef's-tasting menu. L'Etoile currently works with sixteen Wisconsin creameries, including Carr Valley, Uplands Cheese, Saxon Creamery, Murphy Farms, Holland's Family Cheese, and Hidden Springs Creamery. Some labels are very micro and lesser known, such as Fayette Creamery, under Darlington's Brunkow Cheese label.

At Estrellon, the group's tapas concept, the Wisconsin Cheese Board features three rotating selections of cheese along with breadsticks and quince. Graze is L'Etoile's younger, more casual sibling, with a wall of windows looking out to the state capitol building from its perch on Capitol Square, in the same block as L'Etoile. Fried Hook's Cheese Curds are a popular order, as is the Double Cheese Smash Burger on a toasted duck-fat bun, plus the Mac N' Cheese features Hook's 10-year cheddar topped with herbed bread crumbs. Sartori's SarVecchio Parmesan is used in the popcorn starter, with black-truffle oil for additional zest. Sujeo's eclectic Asian menu includes Farmer Johns' Colby pimento in a recipe for Kim-Cheese, a riff on kimchi.

Miller has also competed on—and won—the Food Network's *Iron Chef Showdown*. Appearing on the show in early 2018, he demonstrated his recipe for ddeokbokki gnocchi, folding in Willi Lehner's Bleu Mont Dairy Bandaged Cheddar by grating it over stir-fried Korean rice logs. He also won the Best Chef–Midwest award from the James Beard Foundation, in 2012.

The Edgewater

1001 Wisconsin Ave.
Madison
(608) 535-8200
theedgewater.com

The Edgewater's twin towers rise above Lake Mendota near downtown Madison, the stunning reveal of a restoration four years ago that held tight to one of the building's art deco roots while adding a nearly identical one. A new public pier, spa, two restaurants, café, bar, and two outdoor decks—not to mention updated guest rooms—round out the offerings at this hotel, which originally opened in 1948. During the summer months on Friday evenings, live music in the plaza is paired with a Wisconsin classic—a fish fry meal. Come winter, that plaza turns into an ice-skating rink.

Cheese is no exception to the focus on authenticity during a guest's stay. At Augie's Tavern—a cozy, narrow bar that resembles a romantic nook on a cruise ship—the menu includes fried Clock Shadow Creamery cheese curds with a side of chili-ranch sauce. This same dish can be ordered in The Statehouse, open for all-day dining. Other cheese-fueled dishes on property are white macaroni and cheese with smoky Wisconsin fontina and a wedge salad with Hook's blue cheese. Hook's 1-year cheddar also tops Augie's burger, tucked into a brioche bun.

In reopening the hotel, culinary talent was recruited from all across the country, resulting in chefs like Juan Martinez from Little Nell in Aspen, Colorado; James Deptula, formerly of The American Club in Kohler; and Ronald Taylor, with experience at The Ritz-Carlton Hotel in Chicago. Martinez is committed to sourcing as much local food and ingredients as possible, ranging from Wisconsin cheesemakers to Madison's farmers' markets.

Fried Clock Shadow Creamery Cheese Curds

CURDS:

6 ounces Clock Shadow Creamery white cheddar cheese curds

¼ cup buttermilk

½ cup Wondra flour

Vegetable oil, for frying

¼ cup spicy buttermilk ranch dressing

DRESSING:

½ cup buttermilk

1 cup sour cream

2 tablespoons plain Greek yogurt

2 tablespoons white wine vinegar

½ teaspoon minced chives

Dash of freshly ground black pepper

¼ teaspoon garlic powder

¼ teaspoon Aleppo pepper

⅛ teaspoon Sriracha sauce

FOR CURDS:

Submerge curds in buttermilk then strain before combining with flour, shaking off as much excess flour as possible.

Fry curds in oil until golden brown, approximately 1½ minutes.

Cool slightly before serving, with dressing on the side.

FOR DRESSING:

Combine all dressing ingredients, whisking until smooth.

Recipe by The Statehouse at The Edgewater

SERVES 2

Edelweiss Creamery

"MY FATHER WAS A UNIVERSITY PREACHER," explains Bruce Workman, owner of Edelweiss Creamery. "I was born in Texas." His father's career brought the family to Ames, Iowa, then to Wisconsin.

"It was a real culture shock, being a city boy," remembers Workman, who—with eleven Master Cheesemaker titles—has earned the most titles of any American cheesemaker. For a sixth-grade school project he interviewed Dave Roelli (current Roelli Cheese Haus president Chris Roelli's father) and wrote a paper about him. "It was the very first cheese factory I'd ever been in," he says. With aspirations of becoming a chef and enrolling in culinary school, he started his career making cheese at Northside Cheese Co-op, becoming a licensed cheesemaker in 1972.

When he turned fifty in 2003, he snapped up a vintage creamery, which is now Edelweiss Creamery. "It was just a shell of a building. It had been vacant for five years," says Workman, who saw potential beneath the roughness. "I told my wife I'd like to do something different, get back to the mom-and-pop side of the business." Thirty-three cheeses are made here. Workman's son, Ben, after five years in the pharmaceutical industry, helps with the business. "He made the decision (to join Edelweiss) on his own, but the door was always open," he says. His daughter, Hannah, will soon take over the retail store in New Glarus, currently run by his wife.

Three years ago Bruce taught Ben to make Emmentaler. Edelweiss Creamery's Havarti took first place in the 2018 World Championship Cheese Contest. Milk is sourced from within sixty miles, through one supplier.

"Cheese is on our table (at home) every day," he says. A favorite recipe is Swiss hash browns (potatoes with Gruyère cheese): "Oh my god, it's to die for," he says about one of his favorite meals.

Living among other cheesemakers adds a layer of competition. "The Green County Fair has gotten as tough as a contest for cheese as the World Championship Cheese Contest," says Workman. "You've got so many Master Cheesemakers in Green County. We're all just looking for bragging rights for the year—because next year? You never know."

Edelweiss Creamery Fondue

3–4 garlic cloves

1 teaspoon dill weed seed

2 cups dry white wine (such as Chardonnay)

1 pound **Edelweiss Creamery Emmentaler,** shredded

1 pound **Roth Kase Grand Cru Gruyère,** shredded

Juice of ½ freshly squeezed lemon

Cornstarch

1 shot Kirsch, optional

Black pepper, to taste

Nutmeg, to taste

2 loaves crusty Swiss, Italian, or French bread, cubed

Chopped fruit (melons, grapes, pineapple, and apples)

Bring garlic, dill, and wine to a high simmer in fondue pot. Lower heat and gradually add cheese (do not add all at once), stirring continually. Add lemon juice after all the cheese has completely melted. If mixture is too thin, slowly add cornstarch dissolved with a little wine or Kirsch. Keep stirring. Add black pepper and nutmeg. Fondue should be creamy. Bring to a boil, remove from stove, and place on lit burner on table.

While serving, adjust flame so fondue continues to bubble lightly. Serve with bread cubes or fresh fruit (melons, grapes, pineapple, and apples).

SERVES 4 AS MAIN COURSE OR 12–24 AS APPETIZER

Fromagination

12 S. Carroll St.
Madison
(608) 255-2430
fromagination.com

Located across the street from the state capitol building, and snug on Capitol Square, it's fitting that this cheese shop—open since 2007—is also chronicling Wisconsin's history, from the perspective of cheese.

Every employee at this quirky-named shop is extremely knowledgeable about Wisconsin's artisan cheeses, and that enthusiasm shows the minute you walk in. Maybe you need a special cheese for a dinner party that you want to pair with a specific wine. Or you want to support a cheesemaker you just read about who won an award at a competition.

Local office workers, along with those attending the summer-concert series (Concerts on the Square), love to stop in for a sandwich or salad to go—incorporating cheese, of course. Every sandwich features only Wisconsin cheese, in fact. Examples of menu items are the cheesemonger's choice box (three cheeses selected by the store and lots of other goodies) and the Great Wisconsin Sandwich, a mammoth 'wich on three-cheese *miche* (similar to rustic sourdough bread) layered with Roth's mozzarella and provolone, Italian prosciutto, Tuscan salami from Madison's Underground Meats, Genoa salami, baby greens, balsamic dressing, and olive oil. It's so good that *The Daily Meal* named it Wisconsin's best sandwich in 2016.

Traveling through and don't have access to refrigeration? Grab one of the shop's "orphan" Wisconsin cheeses (a small end piece left over from a special order) along with crackers and enjoy in the grassy lawn across the street, in Capitol Square. And because the shop believes in supporting all cheesemakers around the world, you can find selections from California (like Humboldt Fog from Cypress Grove), France (it wouldn't be a proper cheese shop without Delice de Bourgogne triple-crème), Italy (Parmigiano Reggiano sourced from Italy's Emilia Romagna region), and England (Stilton, from Colston Bassett Dairy in the town of Stilton). There's even a stinky-cheese selection that rightfully includes Widmer's Cheese Cellars of Wisconsin's brick cheese.

For bridal showers or special occasions, Fromagination's "cakes of cheese" aim to impress. They are, instead of layered cakes, wheels of cheese artfully stacked and topped with fresh flowers. For example, the Purple Haze cake—with enough cheese to feed 166 people one ounce each—features Roelli Cheese Haus's Red Rock along with selections from Jasper Hill in Vermont, Cowgirl Creamery in Northern California, and a blue brie from Käserei Champignon in Germany. Gift sets and gift baskets of cheese are popular during the holidays.

This is also a great place to stock up on magazines and cookbooks all about cheese, to further your knowledge about Wisconsin's cheese scene. And the food stock spreads well beyond cheese, also retailing sauces, jams, preserves, charcuterie, syrups, salts, chocolates, and dried fruits.

Emmi Roth

DEEP IN THE SWISS-CHEESE BELT of Wisconsin lies Emmi Roth. Lacy curtains and Alpine chalet–like trim on the retail store are a postcard from Switzerland, where two of the company's four founders were born.

Cheese production began here in 1991. A culinary center opened in 2006 with a chef-grade kitchen, perfect for serving pots of fondue folding in Roth's Alpine-style cheese paired with Wollersheim wine (from Prairie du Sac, Wisconsin). A viewing hall provides a glimpse into production. Tony, who runs the Alp & Dell retail store, yodels in his spare time and hosts guided tours.

Steve McKeon is one of Emmi Roth's four founders of the US operation (Gruyère is still made in Switzerland and imported by Emmi Group). The other three were Fermo Jaeckle and Felix and Ulrich Roth, who were cousins from Switzerland. Their family's cheesemaking history dates back to 1863 in Uster, Switzerland, when twenty-year-old Oswold Roth founded O. Roth & Cie. By 1865 he was exporting to the United States and other countries. "We decided to import the technology, not the cheese," McKeon says about the decision to make Alpine-style cheese in Wisconsin. Vermont was another site considered. "(Wisconsin) made sense because of the Swiss heritage and good source of milk."

In 2016 the Grand Cru Surchoix—which ages on spruce boards imported from Switzerland—won best cheese in the world at the World Championship Cheese Contest. McKeon had already retired, but his daughter, Kathy, who works in the company's marketing and product-development department, phoned him with the good news. "Your baby finally did it, Dad," she said.

New to the company is a line of organic cheeses, rare in the artisan-cheese industry. Most of the cheese is made in Monroe, with some in a Platteville plant open since 2014. Roth is also the primary cheese provider to the Melting Pot, a chain of fondue restaurants across the United States. The cheeses are also exported to Mexico, Canada, and the Caribbean.

Roth House Fondue

3 cups (12 ounces) shredded **Roth Original Grand Cru Cheese**

3 cups (12 ounces) shredded **Roth Grand Cru Reserve Cheese**

2 cups (8 ounces) shredded **Roth Fontina Cheese**

2 cups (16 ounces) Pinot Grigio or other light- to medium-bodied white wine

Apple and pear slices

Grapes

Freshly ground nutmeg, to taste, optional

White pepper, to taste, optional

Soak cheeses in wine in a ceramic fondue pot for 15–30 minutes.

Heat cheeses over low for 7–10 minutes, stirring constantly with a wooden spoon. Do not bring to a boil. When cheeses are completely melted, transfer to a tabletop burner.

Dip bread and fruits into fondue. If desired, sprinkle nutmeg or white pepper onto side plates, to dip bread and fruits into.

SERVES 12

Pan-Fried Brussels Sprouts with Horseradish Havarti

3 tablespoons butter

6 cups Brussels sprouts, trimmed and halved

½ cup sliced shallots

3 tablespoons heavy cream

Generous pinch of salt and pepper

1½ cups (6 ounces) shredded **Roth Horseradish Havarti Cheese**

Parsley, for garnish, optional

Preheat oven to a low broil. If you do not have this setting, move rack farther away from broil heat source.

Heat a medium or large oven-safe skillet over medium-high heat on stove top. Add butter, Brussels sprouts, and shallots and stir until coated. Cook for 10–12 minutes, flipping until Brussels sprouts are browned. Remove skillet from heat.

Toss vegetables in heavy cream and season with salt and pepper. Sprinkle Roth Horseradish Havarti Cheese over top. Broil for about 5 minutes or until melted cheese begins to bubble. Garnish with parsley, if desired, and additional salt and pepper.

Serve immediately.

SERVES 4 AS MAIN DISH, 6–8 AS APPETIZER

Harvest Couscous Salad with Buttermilk Blue

3 cups peeled, cubed butternut squash

2 tablespoons olive oil, divided

Pinch of salt and pepper

1½ cups dry Israeli couscous

4 ounces baby spinach

½ cup dried cranberries

½ cup chopped almonds

1 (4-ounce) container **Roth Buttermilk Blue Cheese Crumbles**

FOR MAPLE VINAIGRETTE:

⅓ cup olive oil

2–3 tablespoons balsamic vinegar

¾–1 tablespoon maple syrup

¼ teaspoon Dijon mustard

1 teaspoon dried or fresh parsley flakes

Salt and pepper, to taste

Heat oven to 425°F. Line a baking sheet with parchment paper.

Toss squash with 1 tablespoon olive oil and salt and pepper on baking sheet. Roast for 30 minutes, turning after the first 15 minutes.

Cook couscous according to package instructions and drain. Add remaining 1 tablespoon olive oil.

Mix spinach, squash, and couscous in a bowl, then add dried cranberries and almonds. Set aside.

FOR MAPLE VINAIGRETTE:

Whisk together dressing ingredients. Pour over squash-couscous mixture and stir to mix. Fold in Buttermilk Blue crumbles, reserving a few to sprinkle on top.

Salad can be served warm immediately, or store in refrigerator and serve cold.

SERVES 8

Fig Flatbread en Croute with Grand Cru

1 sheet frozen puff pastry, thawed according to package directions

⅓ cup fig preserves

1½ cups (6-ounce package) shredded **Roth Grand Cru Reserve Cheese**

1 small egg, whisked

1½ tablespoons milk

2 teaspoons sugar

¼ cup chopped hazelnuts

Ice cream or honey yogurt, for serving, optional

Heat oven to 350°F.

Place puff pastry on a rimmed cookie sheet. Cut diagonal-slanted slashes from outside edges of the two vertical sides of the pastry (about six slashes on each side) toward the center. Leave center area uncut. Smear fig preserves in center. Sprinkle shredded cheese over pastry.

Alternate folding pastry strips over the filling in crisscross fashion—right side, left side, right side, left side—repeating with all strips.

Mix egg and milk and brush over pastry. Sprinkle with sugar and hazelnuts.

Bake until golden brown, about 20 minutes. Cool 3–5 minutes before slicing and serving. Top with ice cream or honey yogurt, if desired.

SERVES 4

Sweet & Spicy Sriracha Pizza

2 tablespoons butter

1 cup thinly sliced sweet onion

Pinch of salt and pepper

1 (12-ounce ball) prepared pizza dough

1 tablespoon olive oil

2 teaspoons minced garlic

¼ cup pizza sauce

¼ cup barbecue sauce

1 cup chopped broccoli

1 cup chopped chicken

2 cups (8 ounces) shredded **Roth Sriracha Gouda Cheese**

Green onion slices, for garnish, optional

Sriracha hot sauce, for garnish, optional

Crushed red pepper flakes, for garnish, optional

Preheat a pizza stone to 425°F. If you do not have a pizza stone, assemble pizza on upside-down baking sheet. It will need about 20–22 minutes of baking time and result in a less crispy crust.

Cook butter and onion in a medium frying pan over medium-low heat, stirring until onions are golden and lightly caramelized, about 20 minutes. Season with salt and pepper. Set aside.

On a lightly floured surface, roll pizza dough into a 12-inch circle. Transfer to hot pizza stone and brush with olive oil, then sprinkle garlic over top. Spread pizza and barbecue sauces over dough and top evenly with broccoli, chicken, reserved onion slices, and cheese.

Bake for 18–20 minutes or until crust is golden brown and cheese is bubbling. Let sit for 5 minutes before cutting. Garnish with green onions, Sriracha hot sauce, or crushed red pepper for more heat, if desired.

SERVES 6. MAKES 1 LARGE PIZZA.

Hazel's

Inside the Baker House
327 Wrigley Dr.
Lake Geneva
(262) 248-4700
historichotelsoflakegeneva.com

Dating back to the Gilded Age, when wealthy Chicagoans built mansions along the shores of Lake Geneva, architectural buffs will love being inside the Baker House. This seventeen-thousand-square-foot Queen Anne mansion was built as a summer residence for Emily Baker, on land owned by her father-in-law, which he received while serving as district attorney of Walworth County. Emily's husband grew up in Lake Geneva and held a special fondness for the region. He was part owner of the J.I. Case Company, now known as Case Corporation (and still in Racine today). Unfortunately, he died three years before the mansion was built, but Emily vowed to memorialize him by placing his initials in the entry.

One unique aspect of the design is the sheer amount of California redwood used for the exterior and the roof's shingles. There are also thirteen fireplaces, a grand staircase, stained-glass windows, and inlaid wood floors

In 2010 Andrew Fritz took over the property, moving in with his two children and undoing its previous chapters as a sanitarium (residents tended to be wealthy Chicagoans who considered Lake Geneva their second home), and as a hotel/restaurant called St. Moritz. His restoration is remarkable, turning it into a high-end culinary experience that also includes six B&B-style rooms.

Even if you're not staying the night, the Saturday afternoon tea and historic house tour is open to all. Imagine being served by staff dressed in Victorian apparel! If you are a fan of *Downton Abbey*, this is your place.

Meals at Hazel's fuse in Wisconsin artisan cheeses, starting with the signature Swiss cheese–style fondue and warm pretzel bites with a side of Wisconsin cheese dip, followed by entrees such as "the St. Moritz." This sandwich is a nod to the hotel's earlier incarnation, featuring provolone melted on an English muffin along with grilled chicken and sautéed mushrooms and onions. The Zucchini Carpaccio features shaved Parmesan cheese and is a signature item on the menu, perfect when paired with a view of the lake.

Hook's Cheese Company

COLLEGE SWEETHEARTS TONY AND Julie Hook knew they'd spend their lives together—but had no idea that meant making cheese. It was Tony who launched a career in cheesemaking. But Julie took home the "Best in Class" award at the World Championship Cheese Contest in 1982 for her Colby cheese, going on to win—in that same championship that same year—the overall "World Champion Award" against all other "Best of Class" winners. She is the only woman to win the "World Champion Award" even today.

In 1987, after Tony had earned a business degree from UW–Platteville, worked at a cheese factory in local Barneveld, and managed a cooperative cheese factory for eleven years, the Hooks teamed up by purchasing the current factory, in the artsy town of Mineral Point, an hour southwest of Madison and snug in the Driftless Region. Built in 1875 as a livery stable for the now-shuttered Washington Hotel across the street, its second chapter in 1929 was as a cheese plant, one of four in Mineral Point. By the time the Hooks snapped it up, the other three had closed.

"Almost every farmer was milking cows at the time, and you couldn't haul it very far," due to unpaved roads and a lack of refrigeration, says Tony.

With access to cold storage, the Hooks began to age cheddar, which few creameries were doing at that time. They started with five-year aging and eventually went to twenty-year aging, an industry first.

Then, in 2001, bolstered by success with Little Boy Blue, their first sheep's-milk cheese, using milk from Hidden Springs Creamery in Westby, they shifted into artisan cheeses and selling cheese with their own label on it. The way Tony saw it, "We can make a little more and produce less cheese and pay a little more attention to marketing." Goat's milk cheeses—using LaClare Family Creamery's milk—quickly followed, then a line of mixed-milk cheeses with fun names like Triple Play (milk from cows, goats, and sheep) and Extra Innings (in honor of the one-year aging process).

Growing up on a dairy farm, Tony was one of seven kids. As the business grew, he began to hire family, starting with his brother Jerry and sister Julie, along with two nephews and a niece (Brian, Jim, and Melanie). The transition was a natural fit for most. "When we became teenagers, we worked at farms in the area," says Tony.

As for Julie, today she sells Hook's cheese at the Dane County Farmers' Market and spends time with her grandkids. "For thirty years we were working one hundred hours a week and raising our kids," says Tony.

Farro, Beet, and Fennel Salad with Hook's Little Boy Blue

½ pound beets, washed and trimmed

Salt and pepper

¾ cup farro or pearled barley

1 large fennel bulb

4 teaspoons extra-virgin olive oil, divided

2 tablespoons red wine vinegar

1 teaspoon Dijon mustard

1 garlic clove, minced

1 cup arugula

3 tablespoons chopped, toasted brazil nuts or walnuts

2 ounces **Hook's Little Boy Blue cheese,** crumbled

Preheat oven to 425°F.

Place beets, ¼ cup water, and a few pinches of salt on a large baking sheet lined with aluminum foil. Wrap foil around beets and cook for 45–60 minutes or until a knife easily pierces the center. Set aside to cool until beets can be peeled and diced into ⅓-inch cubes (about 1½ cups).

Bring farro, ½ teaspoon salt, and 3 cups water to boil in a medium saucepan, then reduce to a simmer and cook until tender (about 20–30 minutes). Strain into a colander, shaking off excess water. Spread out on a baking sheet to cool.

Slice fennel in half and remove core. Slice vertically, both bulb and core, into ⅛-inch-thick slices and toss with 1 teaspoon olive oil, ¼ teaspoon salt, and a few grinds of pepper. Roast at 425°F for 10–15 minutes on a baking sheet until tender and slices are golden. Set aside to cool.

Whisk vinegar, remaining 3 teaspoons olive oil, Dijon mustard, and minced garlic in a large bowl. Mix in farro until grains are coated with dressing, then add roasted fennel, arugula, nuts, and cheese. Add diced beets and mix until evenly distributed. Add salt or pepper as necessary.

Serve immediately or refrigerate for up to 1 day, bringing to room temperature before serving.

Recipe by Jenny Buechner

SERVES 4–6

Green Bean Salad with Hook's Triple Play Extra Innings

1½ pounds green beans, ends trimmed

Kosher salt or coarse sea salt

1 large garlic clove

5 teaspoons sherry vinegar

2 teaspoons sunflower oil

1 teaspoon extra-virgin olive oil

1 teaspoon Dijon mustard

½ teaspoon whole-grain mustard

¼ teaspoon honey

Freshly ground black pepper

1½ tablespoons golden raisins, chopped

6 medium radishes, thinly sliced

¼ cup chopped parsley

2 tablespoons almonds, toasted and chopped

1½ ounces **Hook's Triple Play Extra Innings,** crumbled

Cut green beans into 1½-inch-length pieces. Bring a half inch of water to a boil in a large sauté pan. Add green beans and ½ teaspoon salt then cover, reducing heat, and steam for 4–5 minutes or until tender. Run cold water over beans in a colander to cool.

Sprinkle a pinch of salt on garlic, then chop until it is a paste. Whisk garlic paste, sherry vinegar, sunflower oil, olive oil, Dijon mustard, whole-grain mustard, honey, ¼ teaspoon salt, and a few grinds of fresh pepper in a large bowl. Add raisins and let sit for 10–20 minutes.

Mix green beans and radishes with dressing. Once thoroughly coated, add parsley, almonds, and cheese; salt and pepper for taste.

Serve immediately or refrigerate for up to 1 day, bringing to room temperature before serving.

Recipe by Jenny Buechner

SERVES 4

Sweet and Savory
Unexpected and Fabulous Combinations

What's the weirdest thing that's ever been topped with cheese? Nothing is off-limits here in Dairyland. While Portland says, "Put a bird on it," Wisconsin says, "Put some cheese on it." Or, more often, "Put some more cheese on it."

Family-owned Pier 290 on Lake Geneva in Williams Bay serves up classic Wisconsin favorites like the must-have cheese curds, but the watermelon stack appetizer steals the show. Freshly cut watermelon topped with goat cheese, balsamic glaze, and coarse black pepper embodies Wisconsin lake life in every bite. This stack is best enjoyed with a view (left) after a day on the water.

Innovative chefs and growing tastes are taking the classic cheese-and-fruit plate to new levels. Try the Caramel Apple Cheese Curds on page 157 and the Apple Pie with Sharp Cheddar Crust on page 10 when temperatures drop.

Brie and cranberry is the epitome of savory tang, gooey and warm when the weather is cold. Try brie in the warmer months with mango instead. Up the ante on a bacon snack with American cheese in the microwave—no bread or meat necessary. Wisconsin's neighbors to the south have sweetened a savory breakfast sweet in a mouthwatering way. Leghorn Chicken in Chicago created the blue-cheese caramel biscuit, and no one could be mad. This cheese-centric dessert inspires endless possibilities, uniting two of the creamiest delicacies that might just have been made for each other.

Cheese and chocolate might sound obvious. Elevate that heavenly combo with Crave Brothers Farmstead Classics Chocolate Mascarpone Pie (page 21), Chocolate Ravioli with Chocolate Ganache, Goat Cheese, and Raspberry Coulis (page 110), and Goat Cheese Brownies (page 120). Emmi Roth's Fig Flatbread en Croute with Grand Cru (page 43) and Vanilla-Infused Poached Pears with Montforte Blue Cheese Crème Anglaise (page 62) delight and surprise any cheese-loving palate.

Landmark Creamery

ANNA THOMAS BATES AND ANNA Landmark met at a Soil Sisters potluck five years ago. When Landmark shared her dream to launch a creamery, Bates, a food writer, pitched her marketing expertise the next day.

The two are now partners in Landmark Creamery. Landmark makes the cheese and Thomas Bates operates Landmark Creamery Provisions in Paoli, an adorable—and tiny—artsy town. Sheep's milk is sourced from a small farm near Orfordville, while cow's milk comes from family farms in Belleville and Argyle, plus Uplands Cheese. Landmark cheeses are sold at the store, as well as Wisconsin-made summer sausages, jams, and more, plus pottery and lavender. Cheese plates and grilled-cheese sandwiches are also served. "A lot of bicyclists come through and a beer garden is across the street," says Thomas Bates.

"For how small we are, we worked hard to be successful and get our name out there," says Thomas Bates, who grew up in Nebraska and attended college on the East Coast. Nearly twenty years ago she arrived in Madison for a job at the Department of Natural Resources. Landmark ran political campaigns in Washington, DC. "She has Wisconsin roots and came back," says Thomas Bates. Both live in Albany, on small acreages, digging further into farming by growing most of their own food.

Landmark's five cheeses (including Tall Grass Reserve, the only cow's-milk cheese) are made at Cedar Grove in Plain, and fold in milk sourced from two family-owned farms within an hour's drive. Several Wisconsin chefs—including Dave Swanson at Braise in Milwaukee and Tami Lax at Harvest in Madison—have served their cheese since the first batch was made in 2014. Keeping production small means Thomas Bates can reach out to chefs on a whim, offering a batch. The cheeses are also distributed to New York City, Los Angeles, Chicago, and Boston.

The women credit a tight community of cheesemakers for believing in their cheese. "It's a nice small community. We know each other really well," says Thomas Bates. For example, Thomas Bates helps band Uplands Cheese's Rush Creek Reserve each fall. And, to coordinate a delivery to California, cheesemakers often drive their products to one pickup site, "to have more of a Wisconsin-cheese presence on the coast," she says. The female farmers in Soil Sisters, too, have provided support, "to have this totally judgment-free space, to ask a question and not be judged," says Thomas Bates. Many culinary products—like Reimer's pasteurized meat—sold at the shop come from Soil Sisters members.

Tallgrass Reserve Grits with Greens

2 cups water

2 cups milk

4 tablespoons butter, divided

½ teaspoon salt

1 cup stone-ground grits

1 cup shredded **Landmark Creamery Tallgrass Reserve,** plus additional for serving

1 small bunch kale or collards, stems removed and torn into pieces

1 small garlic clove, minced

1 teaspoon vinegar

Pinch of salt

Bring water and milk to a boil in a 4-quart saucepan, reducing heat before adding 2 tablespoons butter, salt, and grits. Cook for 20–25 minutes, stirring until grits are tender. Add more milk if it gets too thick. Remove from heat and stir in an additional tablespoon butter and the Tallgrass Reserve.

While cooking grits, cook greens and garlic until wilted in remaining 1 tablespoon butter in a large skillet over medium-high heat. Stir in vinegar and salt.

Serve grits hot, topped with cooked greens and additional Tallgrass Reserve. Add more salt if needed.

SERVES 4

Kale & Shallot Pizza with Landmark Creamery Anabasque

Pizza dough

Olive oil, for brushing

1½ cups shredded **Landmark Creamery Anabasque**

4 kale leaves, ribs removed and torn

2 shallot bulbs, cut into thin slices

½ pint cherry tomatoes, each sliced in half

Coarse salt, for sprinkling

Preheat oven to 500°F, along with a pizza stone or upside-down baking sheet.

Roll out dough, brush with olive oil, and top with Anabasque, kale, shallots, and tomatoes. Sprinkle with salt.

Bake until edges are golden brown, about 8–12 minutes.

SERVES 4

Cacio e Pepe: Spaghetti with Black Pepper and Landmark Creamery Pecora Nocciola

4 tablespoons extra-virgin olive oil, divided

1 teaspoon coarsely ground black pepper

½ pound spaghetti

Coarse salt

2 tablespoons butter, melted

2 ounces **Landmark Creamery Pecora Nocciola**, grated

Heat 3 tablespoons olive oil and black pepper in a large skillet until it sizzles.

Cook spaghetti according to package instructions until a minute shy of al dente. Drain, reserving cooking water.

Add 3 tablespoons pasta-cooking water and the butter to skillet. Add pasta with remaining tablespoon olive oil and cheese. Toss until creamy, adding additional cooking water if necessary. Taste and season with coarse salt, if needed. d

SERVES 4

Landmark Creamery Petit Nuage, Grilled Peaches, and Balsamic Reduction

1 cup balsamic vinegar

¼ cup honey

2 teaspoons salted butter, melted

2 peaches, cut in half and pits removed

4 ounces (4 pieces) **Landmark Creamery Petit Nuage**

Mint sprigs

In a saucepan, bring balsamic vinegar and honey to a boil over medium-high heat, then reduce to a simmer. Cook for 15 minutes, stirring until sauce is reduced and thick enough to coat a spoon. Set aside.

Heat grill to high. Brush butter on cut sides of peaches and grill until charred, about 4 minutes.

On each plate, place one grilled peach half and one piece of Petit Nuage. Drizzle with balsamic reduction. Garnish with mint sprigs.

SERVES 4

Montforte

INSIDE A FORMER ICE-CREAM factory in the tiny (pop. 718) village of Montfort, in Iowa and Grant counties, this blue-cheese maker consistently earns accolades, including a "Best in Class" award in the 2006 World Championship Cheese for its Montforte Gorgonzola. That same year, Montforte Blue won first in its class at the American Cheese Society's competition. Ever since, the creamery's two cheeses have racked up medals and ribbons at competitions, too many to count. More recently, Montforte Blue won first place in the 2017 US Championship Cheese Contest's "Blue Veined Cheese" category, and a gold for its Gorgonzola at the International Cheese Awards in 2018.

Directing the cheesemaking process is France-born Christophe Megevand, who also makes cheese at Yellow Door Creamery in Turtle Lake, in northern Wisconsin. But the creamery's true roots date back to local dairy farmers (Wisconsin Farmers Union Specialty Cheese Company) who produced that cheese for the 2006 win. It was later acquired in 2009 by Schuman Cheese, the cheese-import company in New Jersey that also manages Yellow Door Creamery in Wisconsin.

Unlike cheddar, Colby, and Swiss—three examples of cheeses that have been produced in Wisconsin for decades, if not a century—blue and Gorgonzola cheese production is on the rise. More than ever before, Wisconsin cheesemakers are turning to blue cheese, perhaps to satisfy the palates of consumers who are in love with the rich, creamy style that you can only find in a blue-veined cheese. Chefs love it, too: At American Bachelor in Minneapolis, whose chef won the James Beard Award in 2017, the Bibb salad features Montforte Blue. Dierks Bentley's Whiskey Row in Nashville—opened by country-music star Dierks Bentley in 2017—serves up sliders topped with bacon and Montforte Blue. And at Great Lakes Brewing Co. in Cleveland, a pizza on the menu is topped with Montforte Blue, along with leeks, mushrooms, fresh rosemary, garlic oil, and mozzarella.

Both of Montforte's cheeses are crafted rBGH-free milk, which means the cows are not injected with hormones. The blue cheese is aged in a cave for sixty days, while the Gorgonzola is aged for ninety days. Both the blue and Gorgonzola are sold in a wheel as well as crumbles (perfect for topping salads or a steak).

Vanilla-Infused Poached Pears with Montforte Blue Cheese Crème Anglaise

POACHED PEARS:

4 cups water

1 cup red wine

2½ cups sugar

1 vanilla bean, split lengthwise

4 Bosc pears, peeled and bottoms cut (keep stems on)

BUTTERFLY TEA:

½ cup water

⅛ cup butterfly tea flowers

CRÈME ANGLAISE:

1 cup milk

1 cup **Montforte Blue Cheese crumbles**

2 tablespoons sugar

3 egg yolks

Bring water, red wine, sugar, and vanilla bean to a boil in a large saucepan. Lower pears into boiling water and adjust heat to simmering. Turn pears every 5 minutes until they meet little resistance when prodded with a thin-bladed knife, usually 10–20 minutes. Turn off heat and cool slightly in liquid.

Prepare butterfly tea by boiling water and adding butterfly tea flowers. Set aside to steep, keeping tea warm.

Bring milk and Montforte Blue crumbles to a boil in a medium saucepan over medium-high heat. Stir in sugar. Remove from heat.

Whisk egg yolks in a medium bowl and add half the crème anglaise, a small amount at a time. Return to saucepan and simmer over very low heat, whisking for 5 minutes.

To serve, add 1 tablespoon butterfly tea to each bowl, place a pear in tea, and top with ⅓ cup crème anglaise.

SERVES 4

Stroopwafel Cookie Sandwich with Creamy Montforte Gorgonzola & Grilled Figs Drizzled with Citrus Honey Reduction

ORANGE HONEY SYRUP:

1 cup honey

1 cup orange juice

1 tablespoon orange zest

¼ cup lemon juice

8 stroopwafels

4 ounces **Montforte Gorgonzola,** sliced

4 fresh figs, sliced and halved

In a heavy saucepan, simmer honey, orange juice, orange zest, and lemon juice, stirring occasionally for 20–25 minutes until reduced enough to coat the back of a spoon. Syrup can be prepared in advance and refrigerated.

Heat a cast-iron skillet over medium-high heat and grill figs for 2–3 minutes on both sides or until caramelized. Set aside.

To assemble, place a stroopwafel cookie onto each plate and top with a 1-ounce slice of Montforte Gorgonzola. Place another stroopwafel cookie on top. Top with two grilled fig halves and generously drizzle with citrus honey reduction.

SERVES 4

Nordic Creamery

EVERY SATURDAY JUST AFTER MIDNIGHT, Sarah and Al Bekkum load up their van with cheese and drive five hours to Chicago, returning that evening to their farm in the Driftless Region.

The ten-hour round-trip journey to the Green City Market in Chicago is worth it, says Al, because that's their largest customer base. Local chefs and residents have been buying their sheep's milk cheese for years. Four Seasons Hotel Chicago serves pats of Nordic Creamery's butter with all room-service orders. "That hotel," says Bekkem, was the first to take on our product."

After working at area creameries, including Westby Creamery, Bekkum yearned to go out on his own. Today fifteen cheeses are made by Bekkum, who stumbled upon cheesemaking by accident after being laid off from a construction job in the 1980s. "I've been in this industry ever since," he says. Outside of a stint managing a cheese plant in Ohio, he's never left Westby. He's won numerous awards including, most recently, first place in the 2018 World Championship Cheese Contest for Garlic and Basil Butter.

His wife, Sarah, is a partner in the creamery. "She is very much my right hand," he says. Two of their six kids already work for Nordic Creamery, as do local Amish. The Bekkums are the first to make cheese on Sarah's 102-year-old family farm, with sheep's milk sourced from a local Amish farm. "We use small family farms—less than fifty cows—for all of our milk," he says. "We were actually milking our own cows up until a year and a half ago." Their cheese and butter is always on the table at home, a quick walk from the creamery and on the same property.

The Bekkums encourage their kids to explore beyond the Driftless Region; they can always come back. "It's a big world out there and we're just a sliver of it," he says.

Visitors can purchase cheese at the retail store, as well as scoops of ice cream, to enjoy on the deck overlooking the Bekkums' farm and the rolling hills that have made the Driftless Region such a desirable destination.

Quick Cheddar Garlic Biscuits

2 cups biscuit mix

1 cup shredded **Nordic Creamery Cheddar cheese**

⅔ cup milk

4 tablespoons butter

¼ teaspoon garlic powder

Preheat oven to 450°F. Grease a baking sheet.

Mix biscuit mix, cheese, and milk in a bowl using a wooden spoon until soft and doughy.

Drop spoonfuls of batter onto baking sheet.

Bake until biscuits are lightly browned and cooked through, 8–10 minutes.

Melt butter and garlic powder in a saucepan over low heat, about 5 minutes. Brush garlic butter over cooked biscuits.

SERVES 10

Roasted Cherry-Tomato Salad

4 cups grape tomatoes

4 garlic cloves, sliced

2 tablespoons extra-virgin olive oil

Salt and pepper, to taste

1½ cups dry pasta

6 ounces **Nordic Creamery Sheep Milk Feta,** cubed

1–2 cups zesty Italian dressing

Preheat oven to 450°F. Line a baking sheet with aluminum foil.

In a bowl, drizzle olive oil over tomatoes and garlic and toss until evenly coated. Season to taste with salt and pepper, then spread evenly onto baking sheet.

Bake tomatoes until skins pop and start to brown, 15–20 minutes.

While tomatoes are cooling, cook pasta according to package instructions and drain.

Mix pasta, tomatoes, feta, and Italian dressing in a bowl.

Serve immediately.

SERVES 4

"This is my favorite use of Sheep Milk Feta," says Sarah Bekkum. "This just screams summer!"

Smoked Cheddar Cheese Frittata with Broccoli & Sun-Dried Tomato

1 onion, finely chopped

3 tablespoons **Nordic Creamery Harvest** or **Summer Butter**

4 garlic cloves, minced

2 broccoli crowns, trimmed and cut into small pieces

½ teaspoon kosher salt

¼ teaspoon freshly ground pepper

1 teaspoon smoked hot Hungarian paprika

2 teaspoons herbes de Provence or Italian seasoning

¼ cup dry vermouth or dry sherry

½ cup chopped sun-dried tomatoes, preferably in jar with oil

6 eggs, beaten

½ cup whole milk

3 ounces **Nordic Creamery Smoked Cow Cheddar** or **Smoked Muenster Cheese,** shredded

Preheat oven to 375°F.

Cook onion in butter in a 10-inch, oven-safe skillet over medium heat until it begins to caramelize, 6 minutes. Add garlic and cook for 1 minute or until fragrant, then add broccoli and season with salt, pepper, paprika, and herbes de Provences. Add vermouth or sherry and cook until most of the liquid has evaporated.

Sauté sun-dried tomatoes for 2 minutes or until they begin to rehydrate.

In a separate bowl, beat eggs with milk and a pinch of salt and pepper until well combined. Pour egg mixture over broccoli and sun-dried tomatoes. Stir to combine.

Sprinkle with cheese and bake for 10–15 minutes or until eggs have set and top of frittata is slightly browned.

Remove from oven and let stand 5 minutes before serving.

Recipe by Chestnut Street Inn, Sheffield, Illinois

SERVES 8

Roelli Cheese Haus

FOURTH-GENERATION CHEESEMAKER CHRIS Roelli not only resurrected the family's creamery, he brought that slice of agricultural history back to Lafayette County.

Its retail store along a rural highway sells Roelli Cheese Haus cheeses, including the award-winning Alpine-style Little Mountain, named best cheese in America at the American Cheese Society's competition in 2016. Visitors can also grab signature sandwiches like Roelli's Premium Ham Sandwich (Swiss, ham, and mayo on marbled rye). Cheeses are made in back. Chris still runs to a local dairy most mornings to pick up milk.

Chris likes to cook with his cheeses at home. "I put the Dunbarton Blue inside the burger, so it doesn't melt off," says Chris. That cheese represents his hardest work to date. "It was a secret project. At that point, you don't know what you have but you're putting all your eggs in it," he says. Willi Lehner at Bleu Mont Dairy aged the cheese. "I wouldn't be where I am now if it weren't for Willi," says Chris. Little Mountain arrived in 2016, the same year it won best cheese in America. All four cheeses he's made that are distributed have won awards—Little Mountain, Red Rock, Dunbarton Blue, and Haus Select Cheddar.

The family's factory—which made commodity cheese, mostly blocks of cheddar and cheese curds—closed in 1991, faced with terrible market conditions and the pending expense of new equipment. Chris, who worked with his father there during the 1980s and also got his cheesemaker license, reopened it in 2006—but with a twist. Only artisan cheese is made, mirroring the success he saw with other cheesemakers. "If you're not evolving with it, you just get swallowed up," he says. Chris's father still pops in from time to time.

"I never really gave up on the cheese. I was able to drum up the interest of the rest of the family," says Chris. "What I found when I started making cheese again is our name recognition never had really gone away."

Chris's wife, Kristine, works alongside him, helping in the office with retail, accounting, and wholesale. "My passion is making the cheese," says Chris, who uses only one milk source, a fourth-generation family-owned farm. "We know the milk really well and have control from cow to consumer." Chris's cousin Jason handles truck deliveries. "It takes a lot of specific talents to run a small business these days. We've had a head start—three successful generations in front of us. I kind of look at that as my toolbox."

Chris's great-grandfather Adolph, the youngest of thirteen kids, learned to make cheese in the 1700s in the Swiss Emmental Valley. A famine in Switzerland gave farmers two choices: Wisconsin or Russia. When a friend picked Russia, he immediately wrote to Adolph 'Don't come.'"

Red Rock Ham Salad Canapes

2 cups diced smoked ham

12 ounces **Roelli Red Rock cheese,** diced (2 cups)

½ cup diced cornichons

½ cup mayonnaise

1 tablespoon Dijon mustard

1 bunch scallions or green onions, finely chopped

24 rye crackers

Pulse ham, Red Rock cheese, and cornichons in a food processor until combined. Transfer to a medium bowl. Stir in mayonnaise, Dijon mustard, and half the scallions.

Serve on rye crackers. Garnish with remaining scallions.

Recipe by Evan Daniells, chef at the Merchant in Madison

MAKES 24 APPETIZERS

Uplands Cheese

"WE'RE IN THE THICK OF CALVING RIGHT NOW," says Andy Hatch, thirty-seven, and co-owner of Uplands Cheese. It's a spring day and another season is unfolding at the Dodgeville farmstead.

In 2014 Hatch, his wife, Caitlin, and another couple (Scott and Liana Mericka) acquired Uplands Cheese from founders Mike Gingrich and Matt and Dan Patenaude. Hatch had been their cheesemaker the seven years prior. Pleasant Ridge Reserve—the creamery's flagship Alpine-style cheese, aged for up to twenty-four months and a three-time winner at the American Cheese Society's competition—has been in production since 2000.

Rush Creek Reserve, sold only in November and December, was born in 2010. Milk to make this cheese, fashioned after Vacherin Mont d'Or, is sourced during a narrow six-week window each fall when cows graze on hay. "It's really a kind of indulgent purchase," admits Hatch, "with a decadent, custard-like texture." Many families have shared stories of serving this at Thanksgiving dinner.

Hatch sought out cheesemaking experience via global travels in his twenties. "I spent a couple of years in Northern Europe (Norway, Austria, Italy, and France) as an apprentice," explains Hatch. "Those were (my) wanderlust years." Back home in Wisconsin, he studied dairy science at UW–Madison and eventually found his way to Uplands Cheese.

Life on the farmstead is a far cry from Hatch's upbringing in a Milwaukee suburb. But he wasn't raised on steak and potatoes. He was raised by adventurous eaters. "My parents lived abroad. We had a lot of fondue at home," he recalls. "Larry's Market was the only place you could buy Gruyère and Comte." These days, he swaps out the Gruyère for Pleasant Ridge Reserve. "We have a lot of fondue with our kids," he says. "It's a wonderful melting cheese." Omelets, he says, are well suited for Pleasant Ridge Reserve, too.

A border collie and a shepherd-mix dog help move the herd on this working dairy farm. Hatch's wife is a watercolor artist. Each winter she creates a limited-edition poster for their cheese, distributed to customers.

Proof he's come full circle since those cheese forays in Europe? "Now we sell a little bit of our cheese in Europe," says Hatch, pointing to cheese shops in London, Paris, Madrid, and Brussels. "They want to look a little bit avant-garde by selling American cheese. It was pretty much unheard of until a few years ago."

Gougères

1 cup water

6 tablespoons butter, cut into small pieces

1 teaspoon salt

⅛ teaspoon freshly ground black pepper

Pinch of nutmeg

1 cup sifted all-purpose flour

4 eggs

1 cup grated **Uplands Cheese Pleasant Ridge Reserve** (reserve some for garnish)

1 egg, beaten with ½ teaspoon water

Preheat oven to 425°F. Grease a baking sheet.

Bring water to a boil in a 1½-quart saucepan and cook butter, salt, pepper, and nutmeg until butter is melted. Remove from heat and add flour. Beat vigorously with a wooden spatula or spoon. Continue to beat over moderately high heat for 1–2 more minutes, until mixture pulls away from sides of the pan and the spoon, forms a mass, and begins to form a film on the bottom.

Remove from heat. Break an egg into a well in the center (make one with a wooden spoon) and beat until absorbed. Add remaining eggs, one at a time, taking more time with third and fourth eggs. Beat until blended before adding cheese. Adjust the seasonings, if necessary.

Drop tablespoonfuls of dough 1 inch in diameter and ½ inch high onto baking sheet. Using a pastry brush, paint each puff with egg-water mixture then sprinkle with a pinch of cheese. Bake for 20 minutes, until doubled in size, golden brown, and firm to the touch.

Remove from oven and pierce the side of each puff with a sharp knife. Turn off oven and place baking sheet inside, leaving door ajar, for 10 minutes. Cool on a wire rack before serving.

Recipe by Mike and Carol Gingrich

Makes 24 appetizers

Rhubarb, Bacon, and Onion Compote on Toast

4 slices bacon, diced

2 cups sliced sweet onion

2 cups diced red rhubarb

3 tablespoons apple cider vinegar

½ cup packed light brown sugar

Pinch of ground cinnamon

Pinch of ground cardamom

1 teaspoon chopped fresh chives

1 teaspoon chopped fresh parsley

8-ounce whole-wheat baguette, sliced into 24 (½-inch) slices

(1½ pounds) **Uplands Cheese Pleasant Ridge Reserve**

Cook bacon in a large skillet over medium-high heat until brown and crisp. Stir in onion to pick up browned bits on bottom of pan. Cook for 8–10 more minutes on medium-low heat, until onion is soft and slightly caramelized. Stir in rhubarb, vinegar, brown sugar, cinnamon, and cardamom over medium-low heat for 5–8 minutes or until rhubarb is soft. Spoon compote into a container, adding chives and parsley, and refrigerate until cool.

Heat oven to 375°F. Toast baguette slices on a baking sheet for 3–5 minutes. Place one wedge of Pleasant Ridge Reserve on each slice and top with 2 tablespoons compote. Serve at room temperature.

Recipe by Tory Miller of L'Etoile, Graze, Sujeo, and Estrellon in Madison

MAKES 24 APPETIZERS

Salt Roasted Fingerlings with Uplands Cheese Pleasant Ridge Reserve, Arugula Pesto, Roasted Brussels Sprouts, and Guanciale

SALT ROASTED FINGERLING POTATOES:

1 pound fingerling potatoes

1 cup kosher salt

2 bay leaves

4 sprigs fresh thyme

½ cup plus 2 tablespoons extra-virgin olive oil, divided

2 tablespoons sherry vinegar

½ cup shredded **Uplands Cheese Pleasant Ridge Reserve**

½ pound Brussels sprouts, stemmed and quartered

ARUGULA (OR OTHER BITTER GREEN) PESTO:

½ pound arugula greens

4 garlic cloves

2 tablespoons Dijon mustard

2 tablespoons sherry vinegar

2 ounces toasted pecans

½ teaspoon salt

¼ cup shredded **Uplands Cheese Pleasant Ridge Reserve**

¾ cup extra-virgin olive oil

2 ounces Guanciale or Pancetta

FOR SALT ROASTED FINGERLING POTATOES:

Heat oven to 400°F.

Wash and dry potatoes. Distribute kosher salt across bottom of a 2-inch-deep casserole dish and scatter potatoes, then herbs, atop salt. Create an airtight lid with aluminum foil or use the casserole-dish lid. Roast until knife-tender, 35 minutes.

Once potatoes have cooled, cut into 1-inch pieces, toss with ½ cup extra-virgin olive oil, sherry vinegar, shredded Pleasant Ridge Reserve, and Brussels sprouts.

Preheat a cast-iron skillet or oven-safe roasting pan to 400°F. Roast marinated potatoes and Brussels sprouts in 2 tablespoons olive oil for 10 minutes. Cheese will develop a nice crust around potatoes.

FOR ARUGULA PESTO:

Pulse arugula, garlic, Dijon mustard, sherry vinegar, pecans, and salt in a food processor. Add Pleasant Ridge Reserve and extra-virgin olive oil and process until smooth. Taste and adjust seasoning.

To serve, swoosh pesto across plate and distribute potatoes and Brussels sprouts evenly on plate. Top potatoes with thinly sliced guanciale or pancetta.

Recipe by Patrick McCormick, Oliver's Public House in Madison

MAKES 4—6 APPETIZER-SIZE SERVINGS

White Jasmine

AS A YOUNG GIRL GROWING UP IN Pakistan, Huma Siddiqui's parents advised her to pursue any—or all—of her dreams. "My father said, 'Women should be able to do whatever they want.' I think the things I've done in my life came from there," she says.

She never imagined she'd be making cheese in Wisconsin, although she remembers fondly her father's souvenirs from trips abroad. "He would bring cheddar—black and gold—home at times," she says. After stints in North Africa; London, England; and now Dane County, Siddiqui founded White Jasmine: four Gouda cheeses spiced with cilantro, cumin, tandoori, and sajji (barbecue flavor). White Jasmine is a reference to Pakistan's national flower and the fresh jasmines her mother always wore in her hair.

Siddiqui's move to the tiny town of Mount Horeb, Wisconsin, twenty-three years ago coincided with culture shock. She'd followed her brother to Madison, bringing her two children. Her accounting background landed her a business-analyst job at Wisconsin Interactive Network. She quickly noticed that Wisconsinites love potlucks. "What I've learned is no matter where you live, if you know how to cook well, you make a lot of friends," says Siddiqui. She threw Ramadan parties for one hundred guests as a way to meet neighbors. "Food and traditions bring people together," she says.

But despite all of these accomplishments, her palate ached for more spice. "I realized nobody uses any spices and I was shocked," she says. Siddiqui quickly created a line of spices. Then came a line of spice-rubbed cheeses. "I thought, 'We live in the Dairy Land. I want to experiment with the cheese,'" she says. "What I didn't want to do is make another cheddar, or another pepper jack." Her thirty-two-year-old son, a partner in the business, creates artwork for the labels and handles marketing.

Siddiqui also teaches cooking classes in the Madison area. "My goal is to really spread the word about spices," she says. "It's really the healthiest way to eat." At home she weaves White Jasmine cheeses into quesadillas, grilled-cheese sandwiches, and chili (winning a couple of chili cook-offs).

Chicken Quesadilla

½ teaspoon whole cumin seeds

1 teaspoon vegetable oil

1 cup chopped green onions

1 boneless, skinless chicken breast, cut in strips

1 teaspoon **White Jasmine Sajji Masala** spice (or any masala spice)

¼ teaspoon kosher salt

½ cup chopped cilantro

2 tablespoons vegetable oil, divided

4 (10-ounce) tortillas

1 cup **White Jasmine Cilantro Gouda**

Salsa and sour cream, for topping

Sauté cumin seeds in 1 teaspoon vegetable oil. Add green onions and sauté for 2 more minutes. Add chicken, masala, salt, and cilantro and sauté for 4–5 minutes, then cook an additional 4–5 minutes on medium heat until fully cooked. Set aside.

Heat 1 tablespoon of the vegetable oil in a frying pan. Spread half the chicken mixture into an open tortilla in the pan and top with half the cheese. Place another tortilla on top, letting bottom tortilla get slightly crispy before turning it over. Heat the other side until golden brown and crispy. Repeat with remaining tortillas.

Serve with salsa and sour cream on top.

SERVES 2

Bruschetta with Olive Oil and Whole Cumin

1 loaf Italian bread, sliced

4 tablespoons extra-virgin olive oil

4 medium tomatoes, chopped

1 cup chopped fresh cilantro

½ cup chopped green onions

1 teaspoon whole cumin

½ teaspoon salt

2 cups grated **White Jasmine Sajji BBQ Gouda**

Heat oven to 425°F.

Drizzle olive oil over bread on a baking sheet. Bake for 1-2 minutes, until edges turn golden brown. Remove from oven.

In a bowl mix tomatoes, cilantro, green onions, whole cumin seeds, and salt and spoon onto each bread slice. Top with White Jasmine Sajji BBQ Gouda.

Return bread to oven for 2-3 minutes or until cheese melts. Serve hot.

SERVES 4—6

"There could be hundreds of different combinations used to create a delicious bruschetta recipe. With that said, here is one of my favorite recipes—the combination of whole cumin with the melted White Jasmine Sajji BBQ Gouda on top of the tomatoes is exquisite," says Siddiqui.

Cheese Bread

1 loaf Italian bread, sliced

½ cup (1 stick) butter, melted

2 teaspoons chopped garlic

½ cup chopped fresh cilantro

¼ teaspoon red pepper flakes

2 cups grated **White Jasmine Cumin Gouda**

Preheat broiler.

Arrange bread slices on a baking sheet. Mix together butter, garlic, cilantro, and red pepper flakes in a bowl and spread on each bread slice. Sprinkle grated cheese on top.

Place bread under broiler for 3–4 minutes. Serve warm.

SERVES 4–6

"One of my favorite foods and not just when the weather starts to get colder. I love this recipe all year-round. It is easy, delicious, and beautiful," says Siddiqui. "I love this recipe with our White Jasmine Cumin Gouda."

Southeast Wisconsin

JUST A FEW MILES NORTH OF THE ILLINOIS BORDER lies Lake Geneva, where iconic Chicago families built palatial homes during the late 1800s, eventually escaping to them during the Great Chicago Fire in 1871. A twenty-six-mile path encircles the lake, where mail is still delivered by ferry and the downtown is lined with boutiques selling handmade soaps, olive oils, and art. Sailboats muscle across the lake in summer, and anglers dip their poles beneath a hole in the icy surface come winter. Resorts encircling the lake serve cheese plates with glasses of wine as a romantic close to each day.

This region also used to be home to hundreds of creameries, families who milked cows and either sold to other cheesemakers or made their own cheese. Now there are only two: Highfield Farm Creamery is a farmstead keen on bringing people back to the land through tours and visits, while Hill Valley Dairy is run by a thirty-something intent on keeping his family's farm alive by using their cows' milk to make cheese.

In Wisconsin's cultural capital of Milwaukee, home to six hundred thousand residents in the city alone and even more in the outlying communities, Bob Wills—who also owns the Cedar Grove creamery in Plain—has resurrected the art of making cheese inside one of the state's most eco-friendly buildings, nestled in the Walker's Point neighborhood just south of downtown. Local chefs love Clock Shadow Creamery's squeaky-fresh cheese curds, along with the state's only quark cheese, on their dinner menus. Many will walk over to the creamery or pop over on a bicycle on a warm day to pick up their cheese. Food tours make Clock Shadow Creamery a regular stop because, thanks to a viewing area, visitors can witness cheese being made. Wills is also coaching the next generation of cheesemakers, including Hill Valley Dairy's Ron Henningfeld.

Pockets of farm-to-table dining are all over the city, particularly at Odd Duck in Bay View, where the menu is based on what's arrived that morning. A cheese board of four selections might include Nordic Creamery's Grumpy Goat or Carr Valley's Airco (mingling milk from sheep, goats, and cows).

Village Cheese Shoppe in Wauwatosa's charming village, Larry's Brown Deer Market in the North Shore, and West Allis Cheese & Sausage Shoppe in the Milwaukee Public Market stock the region's best selection of Wisconsin's award-winning cheese. But there are also grocery retailers with multiple stores—like Whole Foods Market, Sendik's, and Outpost Natural Foods Co-Op—who are unwavering supporters of the state's dairy industry. Visit the cheese counter and you'll see why.

Clock Shadow Creamery

ONE OF THE COUNTRY'S FEW URBAN creameries, Clock Shadow Creamery's perch on the ground floor of an eco-friendly building in Milwaukee's Walker's Point neighborhood speaks to the neighborhood's evolution as an artisan-food mecca. Purple Door Ice Cream across the street is joined by three craft breweries, a coffee roaster (Anodyne Coffee Company), and a chocolatier (Indulgence Chocolatiers).

Owner and Master Cheesemaker Bob Wills was inspired to debut this urban cousin to his long-standing creamery (Cedar Grove in rural Plain, dating back to 1878 and still in the family) after a trip to Seattle and witnessing Beecher's Handmade Cheese. Clock Shadow Creamery opened in 2012, under the shadows of the neighborhood's Allen-Bradley Clock Tower. "There had never been a cheese factory here and I thought Milwaukee needed one," says Wills, who was born on Milwaukee's south side and grew up in its western suburbs. "By being out in Plain, one of the things we miss is a connection with the customer base."

He also yearned to connect people more quickly to cheese—including curds so fresh they squeak, not compromised via a two-hour car drive from Plain—via a retail shop (selling other Wisconsin cheesemakers' products too) and tours of the glass-walled production facility. His son Bo Wills assists with logistics, customers, and suppliers. A Master Cheesemaker as well as a veteran cheesemaker from Cedar Grove makes the cheese, crafting quark (soft, fresh cheese made from cow's milk and similar in texture to ricotta) and curds, along with Gouda and cheddar varieties. The creamery, which produced Wisconsin's first quark, has won numerous awards—most recently, second place at the 2017 American Cheese Society's competition (Quark with SA Braai Chutney) and, in 2015, third place at the American Cheese Society's competition (pizza-cheddar curd). It's not uncommon, on any given day, for the door to swing open to a group of schoolkids or a food-tour company's group of hungry foodies. From Wednesday through Friday visitors can view production. An average of one thousand pounds of cheese is made per day.

Deliveries to local chefs and grocers are done via bicycle. Four other Wisconsin cheesemakers have launched creameries here, renting the production space until they're solid enough to branch out on their own. They include Ron Henningfeld (Hill Valley Dairy in Lake Geneva), Koepke Farm's LaBelle Cheese, and Anna Thomas Bates (Landmark Creamery in Belleville).

Scallion Cracker with Horseradish Quark, Chorizo & Cilantro Chimichurri

Scallion crackers (recipe below)

3 links Tia Paquita chorizo, grilled or seared

½ cup caramelized onions

Clock Shadow Creamery horseradish quark (recipe below)

Cilantro chimichurri (recipe below)

SCALLION CRACKERS:

1 teaspoon instant dry yeast

2 teaspoons sugar

1 tablespoon water

2 tablespoons plus 1 cup all-purpose flour

¼ cup thinly sliced scallions, green tops only

½ teaspoon salt

¼ teaspoon freshly ground black pepper

1 tablespoon olive oil

⅓ cup cold water

HORSERADISH QUARK:

1 cup Clock Shadow Creamery quark

2 teaspoons prepared horseradish

1 teaspoon lemon juice

1 teaspoon salt

CILANTRO CHIMICHURRI:

1 small yellow onion, diced

1 bunch cilantro, chopped

1 teaspoon red chili flakes

Zest and juice of 2 limes

1 tablespoon minced garlic

¼ cup olive oil

2 teaspoons salt

FOR SCALLION CRACKERS:

Mix together yeast, sugar, water, and 2 tablespoons flour in a small bowl, cover with a kitchen towel, and rest in a warm place until doubled in size. This is your starter.

Mix starter with remaining 1 cup flour, scallions, salt, pepper, olive oil, and cold water in the bowl of a stand mixer fitted with the dough hook until dough forms a ball. Refrigerate for 20 minutes.

Preheat oven to 400°F. Line a baking sheet with parchment paper.

Dust a work surface with flour. Cut small pieces from dough and roll out dough pieces very thin (about 1/16 inch). Transfer to baking sheet and bake until golden brown.

FOR HORSERADISH QUARK:

Mix quark, horseradish, lemon juice, and salt until thoroughly incorporated.

FOR CILANTRO CHIMICHURRI:

Combine onion, cilantro, red chili flakes, lime juice and zest, garlic, olive oil, and salt. Let rest for at least 1 hour.

TO ASSEMBLE:

Slice cooked chorizo. Break crackers into large pieces and spread horseradish quark on each, topping with caramelized onion, chorizo, and chimichurri.

Recipe by Dave Swanson, chef-owner of Braise in Milwaukee

SERVES 8—10

Braise

1101 S. 2nd St.

Milwaukee

(414) 212-8843

braiselocalfood.com

You've heard of CSA—community-supported agriculture where weekly subscriptions to a farm's bounty are sold—but what about RSA?

This is a term coined by Dave Swanson, chef-owner of Braise in Milwaukee's Walker's Point neighborhood, about a seven-minute drive south of downtown. Swanson and his team purchase allotments from regional farms and resell to local chefs, acting as the middleman in the process and helping to create access. It's a solution to all the paperwork, conversations, and other tiny details involved in not only chefs' orders, but also cheese-makers and farmers handling those deliveries to restaurants. It's not uncommon for this administrative work to become "too much" for food purveyors and chefs to handle, which ultimately leads to a breakdown in communications and—sadly—some of these precious gourmet finds never seeing a dinner plate in a restaurant.

After working at top restaurants, including Commander's Palace in New Orleans and Sanford's in Milwaukee (where he was chef de cuisine), and studying at Le Cordon Bleu in Paris, Swanson finally opened his dream eatery in 2011. It's part of what earned him the title of James Beard Award semi-finalist in 2013, 2014, 2015, and 2016. Within a building that dates back to 1907, and became a bowling alley during the 1940s, he took over the entire building, adding a rooftop garden, a cooking-school space next to the dining room, and a few private-dining spaces throughout. Wood from the bowling alley's lanes was reused for tables and flooring in the main dining room. Recently Swanson began reaching out to Wisconsin's Amish farmers, conducting all correspondence by postal mail, given that the population does not use phones or email. This is a testament to his enthusiasm for providing a connection between boutique food purveyors and the diners he serves.

Open for dinner only, Braise is intensely focused on sourcing local, so much that the menu changes daily. Examples of dishes folding in artisan cheese from around the state that might be served during the summer months include heirloom tomatoes with Clock Shadow Creamery quark, and a green-tomato galette with smoked-jack cheese, horse-radish, and sultana vinaigrette. There's also "dirty chai beets"—beets roasted in coffee, with chai reduction, crème fraîche, and toasted walnuts. As a dessert option to close out the meal, diners can opt for a cheese plate with between two and four selections, paired with house-made jam and crostini.

Through the cooking school—in which classes are taught by Swanson, with the help of his teaching assistant—he's also teaching others how to cook with Wisconsin cheese. Classes range from half-day immersions to a semester-long course. One class specifically targets those who love cheese: Cheesemaking, a two-hour primer in making fresh chèvre and goat's milk ricotta at home.

In the summer and fall, Braise's dinners on farms within an hour of Milwaukee are a highly popular event, as is the often sold-out Tour de Farms each September, in which two hundred cyclists pedal to farms that work with Braise along a twenty-five-mile countryside route.

Highfield Farm Creamery

WHILE DENISE WOODS was visiting family in Cleveland, her husband Terry called. He'd bought a cow.

That spun their idyllic farmstead twenty minutes south of the resort town of Lake Geneva—and across the street from the Illinois state line—into a business. Thirty-some years ago they'd packed up their lives in California, moving onto this very property. It was time to make it official.

Terry traveled to Scotland to learn how to make cheese. Then he got his cheesemaker license in Wisconsin. Over five-day stints at the Cedar Grove creamery in Plain—Terry would check into a nearby motel for the stay—and Uplands Cheese Company in Dodgeville, also a farmstead, he picked up more knowledge. Interning at the University of Wisconsin's creamery in Madison alongside a cheesemaker set up this former computer engineer for his life's second chapter.

"It's really a great thing because he makes all the cheese on campus," says Terry. In other words, this cheesemaker wasn't just focused on cheddar or Colby.

A retail store—marked by red-and-white gingham café curtains and viewing windows into the cheesemaking area—sells the couple's cheese, which debuted in 2014. A year later they rebuilt the barn and added a milking parlor. Deliveries are made in a 1930 Model A Ford panel delivery truck featuring Highfield Farm Creamery's logo.

The Woodses speak about their cows as if they are their own children. "They form little cliques. They'll run all around the field and lay down in the grass together," Terry says. They keep calves with their mothers for at least thirty-five days, considerably longer than on a conventional farm.

Denise—who serves on the board of the local historical society—has enjoyed tracking down the property's history, starting with a delivery ticket (for a Sears & Roebuck house) found under the floorboards during a renovation. The farmhouse was built in 1914, the barn in 1911. Armed with a last name, she visited local cemeteries in search of the family's graves to learn more. When she learned the father's occupation, she smiled.

He was a cheesemaker.

Fried Cheese Curds
A Different Approach

4 eggroll wrappers (6-inch square)

6 ounces **Highfield Farm Creamery fresh cheese curds**

2 tablespoons canola oil

1 tablespoon water

"Here is my take on fried cheese curds: no batter or deep frying, and something even the kids can help prepare," says Denise Woods. "This makes a great snack, a side dish with a bowl of tomato soup, or even an accompaniment for cocktail hour."

Prepare a small bowl of water.

Cut each eggroll wrapper into four squares and place cheese curd in center of each (you may have to cut large curds to fit).

Bring up the bottom edge, almost covering the cheese, then fold in two sides, moistening with a dab of water where they overlap. (Water combined with flour will help glue ends together.)

Moisten top edge and bring to center. You will have a little wrapped package of cheese. Repeat with remaining fifteen squares.

In a skillet heat oil over medium heat. Place cheese bundles in skillet using tongs and cook 1–2 minutes on each side or until golden brown.

Cool on paper towels for about 3 minutes before serving.

Recipe by Denise Woods

MAKES 16 CHEESE BUNDLES

Three-Ingredient Cheese Biscuits

1 cup self-rising flour*

1 cup grated cheddar cheese

⅔ cup milk

*Make your own self-rising flour by combining 1 cup all-purpose flour, 1½ teaspoons baking powder, and ½ teaspoon salt.

Preheat oven to 425°F.

Combine flour, cheddar cheese, and milk into a sticky mixture. Drop by large spoonfuls onto a greased or parchment-lined cookie sheet.

Bake for 15 minutes or until nicely browned, turning pan halfway through.

Serve warm.

MAKES 6–8 BISCUITS

"I always use our cave-aged Centennial Cheddar cheese for the biscuits and cheese sauce recipes," says Denise Woods. "In just a few minutes, you can have these out of the oven. They will turn a simple bowl of soup into a warming meal. They're great for breakfast, too."

Five-Minute Homemade Cheese Sauce

8 ounces cheddar, grated

1 tablespoon cornstarch

1 (12-ounce) can evaporated milk

Toss cheese with cornstarch in a saucepan before adding milk, then cook over medium heat, whisking until cheese is melted and smooth.

Serve immediately or refrigerate for up to five days. Reheat in a saucepan or the microwave.

MAKES 2 CUPS

To give sauce a little heat, add a few tablespoons of finely chopped jalapeño peppers or hot sauce. You can also stir in diced cooked bacon or crumbled sausage and serve over biscuits or toast. For a pasta or chicken upgrade, combine sauce with chopped cooked broccoli and pour on top.

"One of the biggest selling points of processed-cheese products is that they will not separate or break when made into a sauce," says Denise Woods. "But in a few minutes, you can easily make a cheese sauce, from real cheese, that will remain smooth and can be poured over vegetables and pasta, and even used to make nachos—a tasty, real alternative to the 'cheese' sauce in a jar. We always have a batch in the refrigerator, so handy for making a quick macaroni and cheese dinner on those evenings we get in late from the creamery."

Hunt Club Steakhouse

555 Hunt Club Ct.
Lake Geneva
(262) 245-7200
huntclubsteakhouse.com

While most come to Lake Geneva to experience "lake life"—including its sandy beach and narrated boat tours around the lake—there is a more buttoned-up food scene to explore. Most of this lies within the resorts, also home to outdoor pools, spas, and golf courses.

Hunt Club Steakhouse, inside Geneva National Resort & Club, is one example. After all, what goes better with steak and wine than cheese? Whether it's aged Wisconsin blue cheese topping a tenderloin or a creamy mac and cheese folding in Wisconsin cheddar (along with New Glarus Brewing Company's Spotted Cow beer), diners get their dose of Dairy State cheese. Two more options are the twice-baked potato with aged Parmesan and cheddar (from Wisconsin cheesemakers) and, for dessert, a rotating special: mascarpone cheesecake with spiced pecans and macerated stone fruits. The mascarpone hails from Wisconsin and is also used to make another special at the steakhouse: housemade tagliatelle with a roasted lobster sauce thickened with mascarpone and served

with summer tomatoes and garden basil, then topped with freshly grated Highfield Farm Creamery's aged stirred curd cheese.

Diners are seated in the 102-year-old Crane Manor and treated to a view of Lake Como (the Wisconsin sibling of the more famous one in Italy). For another look at how the kitchen staff can play around with cheese, book a seat at one of the steakhouse's monthly wine dinners. It's not unusual to see Wisconsin cheeses woven into the five courses, with great pride.

Heather Terhune
Tre Rivali

Inside The Journeyman Hotel
310 E. Chicago St.
Milwaukee
(414) 291-3971
trerivalirestaurant.com

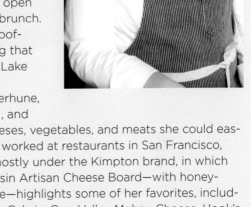

Growing up on a St. Albans, Vermont, farm, where her family grew, canned, hunted, fished, and pickled most of the food they ate, Heather Terhune (a former *Top Chef* contestant) learned to appreciate culinary artisans from an early age.

This enthusiasm drives the menu she develops as executive chef at Tre Rivali, the Mediterranean-inspired eatery tucked into The Journeyman Hotel in Milwaukee's Historic Third Ward neighborhood, with its antique streetlamps and hanging flower baskets. Bistro table-sets on the sidewalk during summer channel Europe while funky floor tile on the interior gets a lot of traction on Instagram. Tre Rivali is open for breakfast, lunch, and dinner, plus weekend brunch. A separate menu is served at The Outsider, a rooftop space with both inside and outdoor seating that wraps around the roof in an L shape, boasting Lake Michigan views.

Milwaukee is still a relatively new city for Terhune, who moved there for the hotel's 2016 opening , and was immediately smitten by the variety of cheeses, vegetables, and meats she could easily source from within a few hours' drive. She's worked at restaurants in San Francisco, Chicago, New Orleans, and Washington, DC, mostly under the Kimpton brand, in which the Journeyman Hotel is included. The Wisconsin Artisan Cheese Board—with honeycomb, house-made crackers, and fruit compote—highlights some of her favorites, including Widmer's Aged Brick Cheese, Montechevre Cabrie, Carr Valley Mobay Cheese, Hook's Blue Paradise, and Saxon Creamery's Big Ed's Gouda.

And if you're a cheese nerd, you have to try the wood-fired Wood Grilled Mushroom flatbread. Mushrooms mingle with Scamorza cheese, which is an Italian cow's milk cheese similar to mozzarella, along with pesto and lemon. The cheese may not be from Wisconsin, but it's still a delicacy.

Hill Valley Dairy

RON HENNINGFELD always knew he'd return to the family farm. The thirty-five-year-old has co-owned (with his wife, Josie) Hill Valley Dairy since 2016, using cow's milk from the family farm to make curds and small-batch cheddar.

He left a career teaching science and agriculture to high-schoolers in Delavan to follow his dream. "My degree in science totally lends itself to cheese," Henningfeld says. "The cheesemaking is a balance of science and using the senses of smell, touch, and sight to direct the cheesemaking." In fact, he even taught students a two-day curriculum in making cheese, with no idea he'd be playing in a vat one day himself.

His brother milks sixty-eight cows at his two-hundred-acre third-generation family farm in East Troy. Henningfeld is the youngest of seven kids. The farm has always operated as a dairy farm, beginning with his grandparents.

Josie "plays a role with everything outside of the cheese production," explains Henningfeld, including social media, selling at local farmers' markets, and marketing. The couple also has two young children; moving into a job with more flexible hours was part of the reason he left teaching.

Henningfeld credits Clock Shadow Creamery in Milwaukee for inspiring cheesemakers like him. After a stint as the creamery's manager and cheesemaker, Henningfeld struck out on his own. "I got into cheesemaking as an avenue for entrepreneurship," he says. After an apprenticeship at UW–Madison he worked a season at Uplands Cheese in Dodgeville. "Uplands is a place where I learned the craft and the appreciation for artisan cheese and farm-based cheese businesses."

Today he rents Clock Shadow Creamery's equipment for his own line of cheese. "It really makes it possible to make cheese without the high investment and risk of building or creating a cheese factory," he says. "It's a fun time for us." Next up? He wants to build cheese-aging cellars, to make (and age) Alpine-style cheese.

Open-Faced Grilled-Cheese Sandwich

2 tablespoons butter, room temperature

4 slices sourdough bread

4 slices **Hill Valley Dairy Sharp Cheddar**

4 slices **Hill Valley Dairy Habanero Cheddar**

4 large slices beefsteak tomato

4 thick slices Applewood-smoked bacon, cooked

1 Anjou pear, sliced

A few arugula leaves

Spread butter on one side of bread and toast butter side down over medium to low heat in a cast-iron skillet, adding one slice of each Hill Valley Dairy cheese on top. Cook until cheese melts and is golden brown, then add tomatoes, cooked bacon, and pears. Remove from heat. Top with arugula.

Recipe by Rugan's ("Where Friends Meet") in Burlington

MAKES 2 SANDWICHES

Northeast Wisconsin

FROM DOOR COUNTY'S WATERFRONT PENINSULA on down to the tiny township of Theresa, Wisconsin's northeast corner is filled with cultural influences that have impacted cheesemakers and the styles of cheese they produce.

Those early Scandinavian settlers in Door County continue their lineage today, including Jesse Johnson, who makes Door County Creamery's cheese with goat's milk from the family farm in Sister Bay. Joe Widmer's Swiss ancestors emigrated to the area armed with expertise in making cheese, a tradition he continues today in a one-story building hugging the Rock River a block off downtown. Widmer's Cheese Cellars is a big name in the cheese world, having won many awards, and could not be in a humbler location.

When, in the 1970s, the Auricchios emigrated to Green Bay from Italy, they had no idea it would be for more than a few years. BelGioioso, which means "beautiful and joyous" in Italian, is now on its second generation of leadership and crafting Italian cheeses that consistently win awards, even over their competitors in Italy.

Inspiring the region to engage in more agritourism is LaClare Family Creamery, a successful second chapter (as a cheesemaker) at this family-owned goat farm. Scoops of goat's milk gelato and restaurant-quality meals are served in the café. Visitors can view the cheesemaking process through a glass window and even see cheese wheels aging.

Locals are committed to supporting local farmers and agriculture, whether that's cherry and apple orchards in Door County or organic vegetable farms surrounding the harbor towns of Port Washington and Sheboygan. The company town of Kohler remains one of the few company towns left in America, where almost every resident has something to do with plumbing and kitchen and bath fixtures. In 1873 the company was founded by an Austrian immigrant, shadowing the wave of cheesemakers who would flock here from Europe over the next century. Today you can enjoy one of the state's finest selections of Wisconsin artisan cheese at The Immigrant Restaurant, tucked into The American Club, a posh resort owned by Kohler.

BelGioioso

MOVING TO GREEN BAY FROM ITALY in 1979 gave Errico Auricchio culture shock. An Italian community didn't exist there. Nor did Gorgonzola.

But this fourth-generation cheesemaker and BelGioioso founder—along with his wife and three small children (then, later, cheesemaker friend Gianni Toffolon)—persisted. Tasked with starting up a US branch of the cheese company he worked for in Italy, "he thought this location was the best because of the vicinity of the milk producers and the farms that produce it," says his daughter, Sofia Auricchio Krans, age forty-one. The idea was to get the company started and return to Italy. But it took three years—and by that time everyone had fallen in love with Wisconsin.

Toffolon is one of the company's eight Master Cheesemakers—the highest number at any creamery—and has been making cheese at BelGioioso (which means "beautiful and joyous" in Italian) for thirty-nine years, since the beginning. He arrived at the age of twenty-three and knew very little English. Provolone was the first cheese he made in Wisconsin.

"I tend to like cheeses that are the most challenging to make," he says, like American Grana and creamy Gorgonzola. Many BelGioioso cheeses have won awards, including eight awards at the 2018 World Championship Cheese Contest, including four gold medals (Parmesan, La Bottega di BelGioioso CreamyGorg, Mascarpone, and Fresh Mozzarella). Another award-winner, Crescenza-Stracchino, placed third in its category in the 2017 American Cheese Society's contest. "It's a cheese that melts beautifully," says Krans. "It's really milky and tangy."

"I don't think cheesemaking is about making cheese," says Toffolon. "I want to make art. I want to be an artist. It's like a sculpture in my mind."

After working at a Green Bay architecture firm, Krans—who attended college in Miami—joined BelGioioso. That was about fifteen years ago. "I actually never realized I'd be in the family business," she says, but the industry's collapse after 9/11 and realizing consulting didn't mesh with her extroverted personality resulted in this happy accident. She and her husband have two daughters (eleven and thirteen). Her brother, Gaetano, serves as executive vice president, and her sister, Francesca, heads up operations.

Sales calls are often hosted at the family's dining-room table—paired with cheese, of course. "My mom is an incredible cook," says Krans. "Our brokers become almost like family." Krans's mother—who grew up in Cremona—always made rigatoni on the weekends with the kids when they were little. "That was just normal to us," she says. "There's just lots of memories of cooking and being together. As kids, she would pick us up from school and bring us home for lunch." It was a traditional Italian feast that the entire family would enjoy together.

"Food is memories in my mind," says Krans.

Frittata di Maccheroni

22 ounces rigatoni or spaghetti pasta

8 ounces **BelGioioso American Grana cheese,** shredded

4 eggs

Salt and pepper, to taste

Extra-virgin olive oil

BelGioioso Mild Provolone cheese, sliced

Roma tomatoes, thinly sliced

Fresh basil leaves

Cook pasta al dente and mix with shredded cheese, eggs, and salt and pepper.

Coat a 14-inch frying pan with olive oil. Place half the pasta mixture in pan, leveling it out. Top with a few Provolone slices, tomatoes, and basil. Add rest of pasta mixture on top. Fry at medium-low temperature. Flip frittata to cook other side.

MAKES 1 FRITTATA

"It's a spaghetti pie, basically," says Krans. "If you had (pasta) leftovers it was a way to use them and not throw them away." In many Italian families, this is a traditional recipe for road trips, because it does not need to be heated.

Rice Frittata

18 ounces Arborio rice

3 eggs

4 ounces **BelGioioso American Grana cheese,** grated

Salt and pepper, to taste

1 tablespoon olive oil

BelGioioso Mild Provolone or **Mozzarella cheese,** sliced

Roma tomatoes, thinly sliced

Fresh basil leaves

Cook rice al dente, 12–13 minutes. Mix with eggs, American Grana cheese, salt, and pepper.

Warm olive oil in a 12-inch frying pan. Pour half the rice mixture into pan and level it out. Add provolone or mozzarella slices, tomatoes, and basil. Cover and fry at medium heat until cooked. Flip to cook other side. Surface should be medium-brown in color.

MAKES 1 FRITTATA

Fennel Salad with Artigiano

½ cup thinly sliced raw fennel

¼ cup fresh lemon juice

¼ cup extra-virgin olive oil

2 cups mixed-greens salad

Salt and pepper, to taste

Toasted pine nuts or almonds

1 orange, cut into bite-size pieces

½ cup **BelGioioso Artigiano cheese,** crumbled

Toss fennel with some of the lemon juice and set aside.

Combine rest of lemon juice with olive oil and toss into mixed greens. Salt and pepper to taste.

Add nuts, orange pieces, and Artigiano cheese.

SERVES 4

La Cassata

⅔ cup sugar

5 large egg yolks, lightly beaten with fork

1 (16-ounce) container **BelGioioso Ricotta con Latte whole milk cheese**

¼ cup **BelGioioso Mascarpone cheese**

2 tablespoons all-purpose flour

½ teaspoon baking powder

2 tablespoons orange zest

2 teaspoons Cointreau liqueur

¼ teaspoon salt

5 large egg whites

Fruit and whipping cream, for garnish, optional

Preheat oven to 325°F. Butter a 9-inch springform pan.

Pulse sugar, egg yolks, ricotta, mascarpone, flour, baking powder, orange zest, Cointreau, and salt in a food processor until smooth. Transfer to a mixing bowl and set aside.

Beat egg whites until almost stiff. Gently fold into ricotta mixture.

Pour batter into springform pan. Bake until center springs back when touched, 50-60 minutes. Allow cake to cool before removing from pan.

Garnish with fresh or sugared fruit and whipping cream, if desired.

Serve and store cake at room temperature.

SERVES 8

"It's a traditional cake that's made during the Easter holiday," says Krans. "It's light and fluffy, almost like cheesecake."

Gorgonzola Sauce

8 ounces **BelGioioso CreamyGorg** or **Crumbly Gorgonzola,** cubed

1 cup heavy whipping cream

Melt cheese in a saucepan over low heat. Whisk in heavy whipping cream and heat until almost boiling.

Serve as a sauce for beef, chicken, or pork, or toss with al dente pasta.

MAKES 2 CUPS

"It's a sauce that's very simple to make," says Krans. "It's just two ingredients. I love it on top of a tenderloin."

Wisconsin Cheese Masters

4692 Rainbow Ridge Ct.

Egg Harbor

(920) 868-4320

wisconsincheesemasters.com

Cute and charming as they are, there are at least a dozen farm-stands in Door County that, on a busy weekend day during summer, can be crawling with people. Sure, it's a great place to pick up a cherry turnover or a jar of cherries drenched in amaretto to make a cherry pie at home, but it can be difficult to spend time with the artisan-cheese selections sold at these stands.

Tucked a block off the main drag (Highway 42) through the county's western side is one of the state's best artisan-cheese stores, solely focused on Wisconsin's production. Wisconsin Cheese Masters was opened in 2010 by Jim Pionkoski, along with his wife Katie Harding, who relocated from the Milwaukee area to blissful Door County with the store's opening. The story behind the name is that all the cheeses sold are produced by

the country's fifty-two Master Cheesemakers—all live in Wisconsin. This means you can sample around sixty of the 650 varieties of cheese these Master Cheesemakers craft. (Tastings of a few cheeses are always held here for free, no matter what time or day you stop in.) Every single cheese has been evaluated by the store's employees.

There's even a cheese-of-the-month club, where three half-pound selections of cheeses chosen by Wisconsin Cheese Masters are mailed out monthly, with the exception of June, July, and August due to warm temperatures that could affect the cheese. Employees have fun creating unique shipments that appeal to those who aren't in close proximity to the store. For instance, the "Betta Chedda" box includes cave-aged cheddar, apple-smoked cheddar, and 7-year sharp aged cheddar, for a veritable taste of Wisconsin cheddar. Or, if you love to drink wine with your cheese, the "Wine Pairing Collection" box was built with you in mind, with Montforte Blue, Sartori's Merlot BellaVitano and MontAmoré, and Marieke Gouda's Burning Nettle Gouda (from Holland's Family Cheese).

Door County Creamery

"ALL OF THESE GOATS are about to have three-hundred-some babies," remarks Jesse Johnson on a tour of his Sister Bay goat farm, which provides milk to his other business, Door County Creamery, one chilly spring morning.

Seven years ago he and his now-wife, Rachael, began milking goats at his family's farm, opening a downtown Sister Bay creamery with their milk in 2013. They were still newlyweds then. A retail café under the same roof as the creamery sells goat's milk gelato, goat cheese, bars of goat soap made by Rachael, and a food menu that's made-to-order. Wine by the glass is poured behind the bar, where a wooden built-in has been rescued and refinished. A glass window allows visitors to view the cheesemaking process, when in production. The store also sells Wisconsin-pride clothing, and locally made kitchen gadgets and home decor, mostly crafted by designers and artists.

After stints cooking at restaurants in France and Italy, Johnson—who, as executive chef, also oversees the menu at Waterfront Restaurant in nearby Sister Bay—came home to Door County with plans to launch a creamery. "I knew I wanted to make a European-style goat cheese," he says. The farm's goats (both Nubian and Lamancha breeds) feed on pesticide-free, all-natural hay and travel between a fenced-in pasture and a one hundred-year-old barn. The Johnsons live a half mile up the road, juggling tasks at the farm and creamery. During the summer months, apprentices live in the farmhouse and help on the farm. Jesse drives a new-to-him 1948 tractor.

"The Nubians have high butterfat," says Johnson, "but don't produce as much milk."

His wife left a career as a school psychologist to help on the farm. "I've been up feeding a baby goat around the clock," remarks Rachael, who says the most difficult part of the job is nursing premature goats back to health and, sometimes, watching them die. Two summers ago, the couple added a milking parlor.

In preparing to open, the Johnsons visited goat-cheese producers around the state, including LaClare Family Creamery in Malone ("That was the first place I ever milked a goat," says Rachael) and Dreamfarm in Cross Plains. And because Caitlin Hatch, Uplands Cheese's co-owner, attended high school with Jesse, the Johnsons visited Uplands Cheese for a tutorial, too. Door County Creamery makes nine flavors of cheese, including wild ramp, culled from ramps picked each spring, and truffle and cherry. (This region boasts Wisconsin's most prolific cherry crop.)

Bringing a Sonoma County–type experience to their farmstead, they offer tours three times a week, starting at the creamery and retail store and ending with a cheese tasting—plus gelato and lunch—at a community table at the farm, overlooking the goats in pasture. Faltum is their cave-aged raw-milk cheese.

Chocolate Ravioli with Chocolate Ganache, Goat Cheese, and Raspberry Coulis

DOUGH:

8 ounces egg yolks

2 cups all-purpose flour

½ cup cocoa powder

2 tablespoons extra-virgin olive oil

2 teaspoons sea salt

GANACHE:

16 ounces (2 cups) heavy cream

20 ounces bittersweet dark chocolate, chopped into small pieces

RAVIOLI FILLING:

8 ounces chèvre (goat cheese)

1½ cups ganache

RASPBERRY COULIS:

½ cup sugar

3 tablespoons water

1 quart fresh raspberries (or 12 ounces frozen)

2 teaspoons raspberry liqueur

TOPPING:

Goat cheese crumbles

Mint sprigs

FOR DOUGH:

Pulse egg yolks, flour, cocoa powder, olive oil, and sea salt in a food processor. Knead dough for 2 minutes. Wrap and let rest.

FOR GANACHE:

Scald heavy cream and pour half over chocolate pieces in a mixing bowl. Let sit for 30 seconds and stir. Pour remaining cream over top and stir until chocolate is melted. Refrigerate for 2 hours.

FOR COULIS:

Dissolve sugar in boiling water. Cool and blend with raspberries and liqueur. Strain and chill.

TO ASSEMBLE:

Boil 4 quarts of water.

For the filling, combine goat cheese and ganache in a mixer, then set aside.

Roll out dough and place 1 teaspoon ganache-goat cheese filling 2 inches apart. Brush water over dough between mounds of filling. Place another rolled-out dough sheet on top and press dough together to make ravioli, cutting out with a ring mold or pasta cutter.

Drop raviolis in boiling water for 3 minutes, then remove and drain.

Sauce raviolis with coulis and top with goat cheese crumbles, and fresh mint.

Serves 4

Pappardelle and Truffled Goat Cheese Fondue

2 cups whole milk or goat milk

2½ cups heavy cream

½ onion, studded with clove and bay leaf (onion pique)

1 garlic clove, chopped

4 tablespoons butter

½ cup all-purpose flour

2 cups shredded mixed white cheeses (Parmesan, mozzarella, fontina, and Gruyère)

2 cups fresh chèvre

3 tablespoons butter, cubed

¼ cup truffle oil

2 pounds fresh or dried pappardelle, cooked

Truffle shavings or pieces, optional

Shaved Parmesan or crumbled goat cheese, for garnish

Steep milk and cream with onion pique for 15 minutes. Remove onion pique.

Sweat garlic in butter on low heat, then add flour and cook on low for 10 minutes, stirring occasionally so as not to brown the roux.

Turn heat up on roux and whisk in milk mixture until smooth. If too thick, add more milk. Stir in cheeses and remaining butter, and truffle oil until melted. Toss with pasta. Top with truffle shavings (optional), shaved Parmesan, or crumbled goat cheese.

Serves 8–10

Baked Goat Cheese

1 cup pureed San Marzano tomatoes

3 ounces chèvre

Rosemary sprigs

½ cup whole olives

3 Medjool dates

2 tablespoons balsamic reduction or aged balsamic

1 teaspoon lemon zest

2 tablespoons extra-virgin olive oil

Sea salt and freshly cracked black pepper, to taste

Crusty baguette, sliced

Preheat oven to 375°F.

Place pureed tomatoes on bottom of a 4-inch baking dish. Sprinkle with half the chèvre, then place rosemary, olives, and dates on top. Top with remainder of cheese.

Before serving sprinkle top with reduced balsamic, lemon zest, olive oil, sea salt, and black pepper.

Bake until sauce is bubbling, 10 minutes. Spread over slices of crusty baguette.

SERVES 6

Layered Chèvre Torte

1 pound chèvre

¼ cup olive tapenade

½ cup basil pesto

½ cup pureed roasted tomatoes or sun-dried tomatoes

2 cups arugula

Line the bottom of a serving bowl or container with plastic wrap.

Make layers of torte by spreading on top of each chèvre layer a thin tapenade layer, topped with chèvre, then a generous layer of pesto, followed by another chèvre layer.

Fold plastic wrap edges over bottom. Chill at least 2 hours or overnight.

To serve, unfold plastic wrap edges and flip onto a serving plate, topping with tomato puree, then arugula.

SERVES 8—10

Joey Gerard's—A Bartolotta Supper Club

5601 Broad St., Greendale

(414) 858-1900

bartolottas.com

Bumping up against its fine-dining siblings in The Bartolotta Restaurants group (including Lake Park Bistro and Bacchus), Joey Gerard's is a throwback supper-club concept open since 2012 that celebrates one of Wisconsin's most beloved dishes: Lazy Susan. It comes in two curated selections: The Badger or The Camper.

Displayed on a round wooden plate that spins and is slightly elevated above the table top, on The Badger are the following: deviled eggs, saltine crackers, smoked whitefish, cubed cheese (cheddar and Swiss), rye bread, Braunschweiger, coleslaw, bread-and-butter pickles, and beef summer sausage.

Another starter relying upon Wisconsin cheese are the popovers, baked with Carr Valley cheddar. Steaks are baked in a Woodstone Josper charcoal broiler that reaches a temperature of 800°F. And just like with supper clubs, diners are encouraged to linger, maybe start with drinks and a Lazy Susan at the bar and then move into a half-walled booth in a room with a tropical-fern design on the carpet.

Appropriately, given the throwback theme, downtown Greendale is good company. In 1938 this planned village—along with two just like it in Greenhills, Ohio, and Greenbelt, Maryland—began with New Deal government backing to build a vibrant, family-friendly community that included a green belt of parks and gardens. It remains a desirable community to live in today. In 2012 the district received National Historic Landmark status.

To close out the night, it's recommended you order an ice-cream drink, like a Brandy Alexander, Grasshopper, Golden Cadillac, or the signature Pal Joey (Kahlua, Bailey's, amaretto, crème de cacao, ice cream, and mascarpone).

LaClare Family Creamery

WITH HER PARENTS TOO BUSY milking goats to accept a business award at the 2009 US Championship Cheese Contest, daughter Katie Fuhrmann attended on their behalf.

The Master Cheesemaker seated next to her inspired her to turn the family's goat farm into an award-winning creamery.

"We're kind of in the mecca of the dairy-goat industry," says Clara Hedrich, Katie's mom, who bought the farm with husband Larry in 1978. They owned just two goats, two peacocks, and a flock of chickens. Clara got her butter-making license and the couple toured other goat farms around the United States.

They found they were sitting on a gold mine.

"Wisconsin leads the nation in goat's milk production," says Clara.

Four of the five children are involved, with the youngest "on speed dial," jokes Clara, who recently retired from a career as a high-school agriculture teacher. Larry used to work full-time in construction.

Jessica runs the café and retail store, which sells cheese, gelato, and yogurt. Café meals weave in LaClare Family Creamery products and, through a glass wall, diners can see ten-pound cheese wheels being aged. Anna oversees the goats and milking crew, and Greg is plant manager. As for Katie, she's the head cheesemaker while raising three small children.

Evalon—an aged goat's milk cheese—won "Best of Show" in the US Championship Cheese Contest in 2011, only two years after Katie learned to make cheese. She is the second female to have won. Then, in 2018, the cave-aged Chandoka won second place in its class at the World Championship Cheese Contest, earning a spot among the twenty best cheeses in the world.

Katie worked at other cheesemakers to learn the ropes. She worked at Saxon Creamery, traveled to Holland "to see what the dairy industry was all about outside the United States," and spent six months working at Cedar Grove. She also worked for two years at Willow Creek and collaborated with Chris Roelli on a blue-cheddar cheese called Ziggy Zak cheese.

Clara and Larry encouraged their kids to work elsewhere before joining the business but are thrilled they've all returned.

Through a glass wall, visitors watch goats being milked in the parlor. Clara often leads tours. On a recent visit, she peered in on two two-day-old goats sleeping in a bucket. "They're (just like) babies, with the same sleeping pattern," she says.

Katie uses the family's cheese to make meals the whole family enjoys. 'I love, love the feta on pizza," she says. "With two young boys, they love the pizza. My husband will make it out on the grill." The chèvre, she's found, can be substituted for sour cream in recipes. "For the Evalon, I'll use it anywhere Parmesan is used. We'll use it on spaghetti or on a casserole." Another family favorite is a pesto-ham sandwich topped with melted mozzarella.

Goat Cheese Brownies

1 cup (2 sticks) unsalted butter

4 ounces semi-sweet chocolate, finely chopped

1 cup granulated sugar

3 large eggs, room temperature

4 ounces **LaClare Family Creamery Original Goat Cheese**, room temperature

2 teaspoons vanilla extract

½ cup all-purpose flour

½ cup unsweetened cocoa powder

½ teaspoon salt

FROSTING:

6 tablespoons unsalted butter, softened

6 ounces **LaClare Family Creamery Original Goat Cheese**, room temperature

3 cups powdered sugar

½ teaspoon vanilla extract

Pinch of salt

GLAZE:

6 tablespoons heavy cream

4 tablespoons unsalted butter

6 ounces semi-sweet chocolate, finely chopped

Preheat oven to 325°F. Line an 8 x 8-inch baking pan with foil and apply nonstick cooking spray.

In a mixing bowl, microwave butter and chopped chocolate in 20-second increments, stirring until melted. Whisk in granulated sugar. Cool to room temperature.

Whisk in eggs one at a time until thick and shiny, then add goat cheese and vanilla. Sift flour, cocoa, and salt over bowl and stir gently with a spatula. Scrape batter into baking pan in an even layer.

Bake for 45–50 minutes, until a toothpick comes out with a few moist crumbs clinging to it. Cool completely before frosting.

FOR FROSTING:

Mix butter and goat cheese on medium speed until light and fluffy, then add powdered sugar, vanilla extract, and salt, beating on low speed until sugar is mixed in. Beat on medium speed until light and fluffy.

Spread frosting over cooled brownies in pan. Refrigerate for 20 minutes before glazing.

FOR GLAZE:

Heat cream and butter in a small saucepan over medium heat and bring to a simmer. Pour over chopped chocolate in a bowl and let sit for 1 minute. Whisk chocolate and cream together until smooth and shiny. Pour over brownies and smooth into an even layer.

Refrigerate the brownies until glaze is firm, at least 45 minutes.

To cut brownies, lift from pan using foil. Cut into small squares. Wash knife in warm water between cuts for the cleanest cuts. The brownies are easiest to cut when cold, but for the best taste and texture, let sit at room temperature for 20 minutes before eating.

MAKES ONE 8" X 8" PAN OF BROWNIES

Goat Cheese Layered Taco Dip

8 ounces **LaClare Family Creamery Original Goat Cheese**

8 ounces sour cream

1 (16-ounce) jar mild salsa

½ packet taco seasoning

2 cups finely shredded iceberg lettuce

2 large tomatoes

1 cup shredded cheddar cheese

Using an electric mixer, combine goat cheese, sour cream, salsa, and taco seasoning in a large bowl.

Spread on bottom of a large, shallow dish and top with shredded lettuce, tomatoes, and shredded cheddar cheese.

Serve with baked tortilla chips.

SERVES 8—10

BBQ Shrimp & Goat Cheese Toast

½ pound shrimp, peeled and deveined

1 teaspoon brown sugar

½ teaspoon smoked paprika

¼ teaspoon chipotle chili powder

¼ teaspoon onion powder

2 tablespoons unsalted butter

2 garlic cloves, finely minced or pressed

2 tablespoons barbecue sauce

4 ounces **LaClare Family Creamery Original Goat Cheese**

¼ teaspoon salt

¼ teaspoon black pepper

½ lime, juiced

4 pieces bread, toasted

Fresh oregano and cilantro, for topping

Pat shrimp dry with paper towels.

Whisk together sugar, paprika, chili powder, and onion powder. Sprinkle evenly over shrimp.

Cook shrimp in butter—on both sides until pink—over medium heat in a large skillet. Whisk butter occasionally to prevent burning. Stir in garlic and barbecue sauce.

Mash LaClare Family Creamery Original Goat Cheese with salt, pepper, and lime juice in a bowl. Spread on toast pieces, topping with shrimp, oregano, and cilantro.

Serves 4

Red Barn Family Farms

THE AVERAGE WISCONSIN DAIRY farm is run by only a few people, who pull long hours to milk and feed the cows, ensure there's a buyer for the milk, and do their best to keep the lights on.

Red Barn Family Farms unifies these small, family-owned farms under one brand, employing a cooperative approach. Places like Bearded Heart Coffee—a tiny-house coffee shop in Door County just a few yards from Lake Michigan—and top chefs from across the state are true fans, adding the name Red Barn Family Farms to their menus and signage.

"Our role is to hand-select small family farms," says Paula Homan, who started Red Barn Family Farms with her husband, Dr. Terry Homan, a large-animal dairy veterinarian, "and to pay them a sustainable price based on excellence in animal health and care and milk quality." Through partnerships with three different creameries (Willow Creek Creamery, Door Artisan Cheese Company, and Springside Cheese Corporation), milk is shipped from the farm to the factory and the cheese sold under the Red Barn Family Farms label. Retailers who carry the cheese include Eataly in Chicago and New York City, and Rainbow Grocery Cooperative in San Francisco. Door Artisan Cheese Company in Egg Harbor (Door County) also buys the milk to make its own line of cheese. Mike Brennenstuhl at Door Artisan Cheese Company and Jon Metzig at Willow Creek Creamery in Berlin are both Master Cheesemakers.

One of the farm families linked to Red Barn Family Farms is the Marcks family in Black Creek. With forty cows, their farm is small, but mighty. It's not uncommon to see three or four generations of cow families running around on their farm. Similarly, Neal, Amy, and Steven Holewinski in Pulaski, who run their family's century-old farm, are a boutique operation through and through. Each of their thirty-nine red-and-white Holstein cows has a name, and it's an entirely self-sustaining operation: A cow hasn't had to be purchased from outside of the farm since 1977. Instead, the cows continue to procreate. Also in Pulaski, Bob and Mary Nett have been farming here since they bought their 375-acre farm in their twenties. That was forty years ago. Their sixty-five cows provide "exceptional quality milk," says Homan.

Gnocchi with 'Nduja Red Sauce

GNOCCHI:

6-7 russet potatoes

¾ cup all-purpose flour

1 teaspoon kosher salt

RED SAUCE:

1 (28-ounce) can whole peeled tomatoes

2 fillets anchovies, packed in oil

¼ cup olive oil

3 garlic cloves, chopped

2 ounces Smoking Goose 'nduja (sausage spread native to Calabria, Italy)

¼ teaspoon sugar

Kosher salt, to taste

GARNISH:

6 ounces **Red Barn Family Farms Cupola,** shredded

Parsley, chopped

FOR GNOCCHI:

Preheat oven to 350°F.

Prick potatoes and cook for 1 hour on oven rack in top third of oven. Remove potatoes from oven and peel skins once they're cool.

Put potatoes through a food mill or ricer then onto a baking sheet lined with paper towels to help absorb extra moisture. Cool completely.

Transfer potato mixture to a large bowl and mix with flour and salt until a sticky dough forms.

Lightly flour your hands and divide dough into six portions, rolling each into a long, ½-inch-thick rope. Cut each rope into 1-inch pieces.

Bring water to a boil and add salt.

Add gnocchi to boiling water in batches. When they begin to float (about 3 minutes), remove from water and add to red sauce.

FOR RED SAUCE:

Puree tomatoes and anchovies.

Warm oil in a medium pot, then add garlic and cook until it starts to brown and becomes fragrant.

Stir in 'nduja to help melt it down. Once 'nduja becomes very soft, add tomato puree, then sugar and salt to taste.

Serve with Cupola cheese and parsley.

Recipe by Forage & Foster, a Chicago-based specialty-food distributor

SERVES 6

Poutine with Red Barn Family Farms Cheese Curds

4-5 medium potatoes

Olive oil

Salt and pepper, to taste

2 tablespoons olive oil

1 tablespoon all-purpose flour

1 cup beef stock

Red Barn Family Farms cheese curds

Preheat oven to 425°F.

Cut potatoes into fry shape you desire and mix in a bowl with olive oil, salt, and pepper. Bake for 40 minutes, flipping halfway through.

To make gravy, heat olive oil in saucepan on medium heat, whisking with flour until it becomes a paste. Cook for 30 seconds. Add beef stock and bring to a simmer. Let sit to thicken and add pepper if desired.

To serve, layer fries and Red Barn cheese curds in a bowl and ladle on gravy.

Recipe by Sophia Herczeg

SERVES 4–6

Renard's Cheese

"WHEN I GRADUATED FROM HIGH SCHOOL, I swore I was never going to make cheese," says Chris Renard. But after a food-service job in southeastern Wisconsin, his Door County hometown pulled him back north. Urban living just wasn't for him.

In 1995 he returned to the family's cheese business in Algoma, becoming a Master Cheesemaker and taking the reins—with his wife, Ann—in 2014. Renard hopes his four children (between the ages of ten and twenty-one) aspire to join Renard's Cheese one day, but he's applying zero pressure. "I'd actually prefer they leave (and then come back)," he says. Ann assists with paperwork, and together they manage the factory and their retail stores in Algoma and Sturgeon Bay.

Renard's grandfather Howard Renard fell into cheesemaking by accident. Delivering milk to a cheese factory in the Door County town of Namur when he was fourteen years old, one day he pitched in with production. By age nineteen he was running the dairy and finally bought a factory of his own in 1961. His son, Gary, bought a cheese factory after he graduated from high school and, in 1975, combined his factory with his father's. The retail store and café in Sturgeon Bay was built in 2012 and continues to be a popular spot for vacationers in Door County. "We wanted to make our location more of a destination," Renard says. Customers can pick up fresh cheese curds, order an egg-and-cheese biscuit or Renard's signature grilled-cheese sandwich from the café, or buy a take-and-bake pizza or frozen breaded cheese curds for later.

Twenty-six farms within thirty miles supply milk to Renard's Cheese, which makes somewhere around 50 types of cheese, plus cheese spreads. Chris's parents and grandparents continue to live nearby. Several area restaurants source Renard's Cheese curds for breaded cheese curd menu items, along with other cheeses for sandwiches and signature dishes. In the 2017 American Cheese Society's competition, Renard's Cheese's cheddar cheese curds took third place and its pesto farmer cheese first place.

Renard's Signature Grilled-Cheese Sandwich

2 slices Texas White toast

Butter

2 slices **Renard's Farmers Cheese**

1 tablespoon pesto

3 slices cooked bacon

⅛ cup fresh spinach leaves

Parmesan cheese, shredded

Butter one side each of Texas White toast slices. Lay one slice buttered side down in a frying pan or on a panini grill. Top with one slice of Renard's Farmers Cheese, then pesto, bacon, and spinach, followed by second cheese slice and second slice of bread, buttered side up. Grill until golden brown, then top with Parmesan cheese.

MAKES 1 SANDWICH

Renard's Cheesy Potato with Bacon Soup

4 tablespoons butter

1 sweet onion, chopped

9¾ cups chicken broth

1 quart whipping cream

½ pound bacon, cooked

5 pounds potatoes, peeled and sliced

8 ounces **Renard's Onion & Garlic Cheese**, shredded

8 ounces **Renard's Medium Cheddar Cheese**, shredded

8 ounces **Renard's 1-Year Cheddar Cheese**, shredded

Roux, for thickening (melted butter and flour mixture)

Salt and pepper, to taste

Sauté butter and onion, add chicken broth, and bring to a boil. Stir in whipping cream and add bacon. Return to a boil, stirring occasionally, and add potatoes. Cook until potatoes are tender, about 10 minutes.

Remove from heat. Stir in cheeses until melted. Add prepared roux to desired thickness, then salt and pepper to taste.

SERVES 8—10

Sartori Company

ON EACH WEDGE OF SARTORI cheese is the Sartori family crest—featuring the state of Wisconsin, a herd of cows, and the ship that brought Paolo Sartori to America.

In 1939, he cofounded with Louis Rossini a cheese company in Plymouth, an hour north of Milwaukee, called S&R Cheese Corp. He also achieved something remarkable: He became the first US exporter of cheese to Italy. In 1986 Jim Sartori—Paolo's grandson—took over and continued the tradition.

Today the company is on its fourth generation and amasses many cheese awards, including—for the Black Pepper BellaVitano—Grand Champion in the 2017 US Championship Cheese Contest. Bert Sartori serves as executive vice president of sales while Maria is brand ambassador. Both are Paolo's great-grandchildren. Master Cheesemaker Mike Matucheski has been crafting cheese for nearly 25 years. He still lives on the farm where he grew up, and where he made cheese alongside his grandmother.

"Growing up, we had small cheese plants scattered around the area. I was lucky enough to have family and friends connected to them. But, overall, the stores had mostly commodity or, as I sometimes called it, 'common' cheese. I always sought out what were to me unusual or unknown cheeses. As a college student in Madison, we took 'field trips' to Green County in search of Swiss, brick, Havarti, and Muenster," says Matucheski.

Making cheese is his dream job. "I knew it the first time I hooped cheese at the Antigo plant. I was totally enchanted by the mystery of turning milk into cheese and still am today," he says. Cooking with the cheeses at home keeps him in tune with their flavor profile. "Black Pepper Bella paninis are a staple," he says. "I've been severely into [making] ramen since visiting Japan with my sons last May. And, yes, my ramen has a cheesy broth, and what noodle doesn't need some great cheese?"

Bert and Maria are both licensed cheesemakers and have been involved with the business in some way since they were thirteen years old. But they also took jobs outside of Sartori. "Having outside experience is crucial in order to be able to bring back key learnings and integrate them into the family business with better perspective," says Bert.

They also eat a lot of cheese. "You won't see a family gathering without a Sartori cheese board being the center of the spread," says Maria. "Often it is out as a grazing appetizer prior to family or holiday meals, and our meals are always topped with cheese."

Sartori Classic Asiago Portabella Burger

6 large portabella mushrooms, stems and gills removed

1 cup pesto (store-bought or homemade)

Olive oil, as needed

Salt and pepper, to taste

1 cup **Sartori Classic Asiago**, shredded

6 hamburger buns, toasted

Suggested toppings: chipotle aioli, spinach leaves, extra pesto, or sun-dried tomatoes

Preheat grill or oven to 400˚F.

Brush each mushroom with pesto, adding a little olive oil to loosen up pesto a bit if needed. Season with salt and pepper to taste.

Either grill or roast mushrooms in oven, turning every few minutes until tender, about 15–20 minutes.

Top each mushroom with shredded Classic Asiago and return to grill until melted.

Assemble burgers and serve.

Serves 6

Sartori MontAmoré Cheddar Macaroni & Cheese

4 cups dried macaroni

6 tablespoons butter, divided

¼ cup all-purpose flour

2½ cups milk

2 teaspoons dry mustard

1 egg, beaten

1 block **Sartori MontAmoré Cheddar,** shredded

1 wedge **Sartori Classic Fontina,** shredded

1 wedge **Sartori Classic Parmesan,** grated, divided

Salt and pepper, to taste

¼ cup chopped sun-dried tomatoes, optional

¼ cup panko bread crumbs

⅓ cup chopped fresh parsley

1 baguette, sliced diagonally and toasted

Preheat oven to 350°F.

Bring a large pot of salted water to a boil. Cook pasta for a few minutes (it should be too firm to eat) and drain.

Melt 4 tablespoons butter in a large pot, whisking in flour over medium-low heat until golden brown, 3–5 minutes. Whisk in milk and mustard until smooth and cook until mixture thickens, 3–5 minutes. Reduce heat to low.

Temper egg by slowly whisking in ¼ cup warm sauce; return to pot. Stir in all cheese except ½ cup Parmesan. Season with salt and pepper to taste and add sun-dried tomatoes if desired.

Pour into a baking dish. Melt remaining 2 tablespoons butter with bread crumbs and parsley and sprinkle on top. Bake for 15 minutes.

Serve with toasted baguette slices.

SERVES 6—8

Saxon Creamery

LISA HILL WAS "BIG ED" ED KLESSIG'S care-giver for five years after a car accident left him a quadriplegic. "When he passed (in 2006), I lost my job," she says. "He was my life." But she quickly got another job, handling operations at Saxon Creamery, the Klessig family's new business.

Milk comes from Saxon Homestead Farm, a fifth-generation family business founded by Klessig's ancestors in 1850 that milks Jersey and Holstein grass-fed cows three miles from the creamery. Karl and Robert Klessig and their families manage the farm. Saxon Creamery began making cheese in 2007. Eric Steltenpohl crafts award-winning cheeses that have snagged awards at both the US Championship Cheese Contest and World Championship Cheese Contest.

An illustration designed by Hill as an homage features Ed standing in a doorway at his farm. A fourth-generation cheesemaker, his family hails from Saxony, Germany. Klessig was born in Wisconsin. One of his sons—Klessig had eight children—traveled to New Zealand during the 1980s, to learn how to transition from conventional to grass-based farming.

Hill strongly believes in *terroir*, a French term often used by winemakers. What cows graze on during a certain time of year (for example, dandelions in spring or clover in summer) affects how the milk tastes, adding flavor to the cheese, just as a bottle of wine may slightly taste like the vineyard's limestone soil. "Being in close proximity of Lake Michigan allows for cool nights," says Hill, "and extra moisture in the air, which feeds the grasses that the cows graze on for nine months out of the year.

"Right now, 'the girls' over there are pregnant and calving," Hill says on a chilly March day about the Jersey and Holstein cows that supply milk. They operate a "closed herd," which they have been building for three generations. This means it no longer becomes necessary to buy animals. Instead, they keep the calves and replace older cows.

In the winter, she says, their milk is very rich in cream fat. Using this milk, Saxon makes its Snowfields Butterkase-style cheese, aged for six months and released each October as a winter special-edition cheese.

The cheese wheels feature a beautiful design—a flowing-leaf pattern and Saxon label printed right into the rind, hand-painted using natural sponges, just like in the Netherlands. Each wheel is then flipped seventy times in open-air caves and aged on wood boards. Big Ed's Gouda Style is the signature cheese. It's aged for ninety days in three different aging cellars. Saxon Creamery also makes eleven other cheeses, including three spreads and an English farmhouse style of cheddar called Pastures, bandage-wrapped and aged for between six and ten months.

Alpine Stromboli

1 pound frozen pizza dough, thawed

3 tablespoons butter, melted

Pinch of garlic powder

8 slices **Saxon Creamery Saxony Alpine Cheese,** plus additional for shredding on top

¼ pound thinly sliced pepperoni or Genoa

¼ pound thinly sliced Virginia or baked ham

½ cup banana-pepper rings

¾ cup marinara sauce from a jar or ranch dressing, for dipping

Preheat oven to 400°F. Grease a baking sheet.

Roll dough to a 12- by 14-inch rectangle. Layer ingredients in this order: butter, garlic powder, sliced cheese, meats, and pepper rings. Roll up and pinch seam to seal. Sprinkle shredded cheese on top.

Bake for 20–25 minutes, then slice and serve.

Recipe by Eric Steltenpohl

MAKES 1 STROMBOLI

"This sandwich brings the best in Italian flavors and Wisconsin cheese. It's a hardy sandwich that can feed a hungry crowd. You can add a little extra fun by dipping in ranch dressing or marinara sauce," says Eric Steltenpohl.

Big Ed's Stuffed Mushrooms

24–48 medium to large fresh mushrooms, stems removed and reserved

4 ounces cream cheese, softened

¼ cup bread crumbs

2 tablespoons finely chopped mushroom stems

1 cup finely shredded **Saxon Creamery Big Ed's Gouda**

¼ teaspoon garlic powder

½ teaspoon salt

Preheat oven to broil.

Clean mushrooms and set aside.

Combine cream cheese, bread crumbs, mushroom stems, cheese, garlic powder, and salt in a small bowl.

Stuff each mushroom with a heaping amount of filling. Place on a broiler-safe baking sheet. Broil 4–6 minutes until filling turns golden brown.

Serve warm.

SERVES 6–8

Bacon Cheeseburgers

1 pound ground sirloin

1 pound ground chuck

1 teaspoon salt

½ teaspoon freshly ground pepper

¼ cup chopped mixed fresh herbs (such as basil, mint, and oregano)

6 hamburger buns

Suggested toppings: **Saxon Creamery Garlic & Pimiento cheese,** cooked bacon slices, lettuce, and tomato slices

Preheat grill to 350–400°F (medium-high) heat.

Gently combine sirloin, chuck, salt, and pepper. Stir fresh herbs into meat mixture. Shape mixture into six 5-inch patties.

Grill, covered with lid, 4–5 minutes on each side or until beef is no longer pink in the center.

Serve on hamburger buns with toppings.

SERVES 6

Sausages with Acorn Squash and Onion

1 large acorn squash, halved, seeded, and cut into ½-inch slices

1 red onion, cut into 4-inch wedges

3 tablespoons olive oil

Salt and pepper, to taste

4 hot or sweet Italian sausages (¾ pound)

½ cup grated **Saxon Creamery Asiago Fresca cheese**

1 tablespoon chopped fresh sage leaves

¼ cup dried cherries, chopped

Preheat oven to 475°F.

Toss squash and onion with oil on a rimmed baking sheet and arrange in an even layer. Season with salt and pepper. Add sausages. Roast until vegetables are tender, about 15–18 minutes.

Heat broiler.

Sprinkle Asiago and sage over vegetables. Broil until cheese is browned and bubbling and sausages are cooked (about 3 minutes).

Sprinkle with cherries and serve.

SERVES 4

Bacon and Tomato Cups

8 slices bacon

1 tomato, chopped

½ onion, chopped

3 ounces **Saxon Creamery Saxony Alpine Cheese,** shredded

½ cup mayonnaise

1 teaspoon dried basil

1 (16-ounce) can refrigerated buttermilk-biscuit dough

Preheat oven to 375°F. Lightly grease a mini-muffin pan.

Cook bacon in a skillet over medium heat until evenly browned. Drain on paper towels.

Crumble bacon into a mixing bowl. Add tomato, onion, Saxony cheese, mayonnaise, and basil.

Separate biscuits into halves horizontally. Place each half into a mini-muffin cup. Fill each biscuit half with bacon mixture.

Bake until golden brown, 10–12 minutes.

SERVES 4

Big Ed's Serrano Gouda Cheesy Spuds

3 teaspoons butter, divided

3 pounds baby butter potatoes

1 yellow onion, chopped

2 garlic cloves, minced

1 pound bacon

1 wedge **Saxon Creamery Big Ed's Serrano Gouda Cheese Wedge,** grated

2 teaspoons **Big Ed's Gouda Cheese Spread**

2 tablespoons heavy whipping cream

Melt 2 teaspoons butter in a saucepan. Add potatoes with skins on and fry until golden brown and soft. Place potatoes in a slow cooker for 4–6 hours.

Fry onions, garlic, and bacon until crispy, then layer mixture over potatoes.

Melt remaining 1 teaspoon butter in a saucepan. Add Big Ed's Serrano Gouda Cheese Wedge and Big Ed's Gouda Cheese Spread. Mix until creamy.

Add cream to cheese and stir until smooth. Spoon cheese sauce over potatoes.

SERVES 4

Widmer's Cheese Cellars of Wisconsin

JOE WIDMER'S GRANDFATHER emigrated from Switzerland in 1905 at the age of eighteen, working as an apprentice in a cheese factory. In 1922 he bought his own factory, what is now Widmer's Cheese Cellars and known for its brick, cheddar, and Colby cheese, which have won many awards. Today Joe makes cheese in the same factory, using the same open vats his grandfather once did, to the tune of 360,000 pounds of brick cheese each year.

Across the street from the Rock River in the tiny town of Theresa, the outdoor aesthetic of the factory and its retail store appear unchanged since the 1920s. Locals rush in throughout the day to buy cheese and production hums along, some of it in an open viewing area.

"We still make cheese traditionally. We haven't changed that," says Joe, who is grooming his son Joey to possibly take over the business. "It's not machine made. It's handmade."

Cheese has always been a part of the Widmer family. "My mom used to put aged brick on pizza," recalls Widmer. "And you could smell it outside the house, like Limberger but flavorful as heck." He also likes to use a combination of Colby, aged cheddar, and brick when making macaroni and cheese and grilled-cheese sandwiches.

Joe didn't plan to make cheese. "My dad said to me, 'Do you want to go to school or make cheese?' I said 'Neither. I'm sick of cheese and school,'" recalls Joe. He wore his hair in a long ponytail and worked on the railroad. But after studying dairy science in college, he told his dad he'd like to make cheese.

Widmer's Cheese Cellars' cheeses are distributed to high-end restaurants across the country. Joe goes out into the market often to meet chefs, consumers, and retailers. "A lot of chefs like our Caraway Aged Brick cheese. That's a German tradition. The Germans normally would eat their aromatic brick cheese on caraway rye bread, so we started to make Caraway Aged Brick for them," he says. In fact, brick was invented in Wisconsin in 1877, by John Jossi.

Creamy Brick Spread

8 ounces **Widmer's Wisconsin Brick cheese,** shredded

8 ounces cream cheese with chives and onion, softened

½ teaspoon hot-pepper sauce

Cocktail rye or pumpernickel bread, crisp crackers, or bagel chips

Blend cheeses and hot-pepper sauce until smooth.

Spread on bread, crisp crackers, or bagel chips.

MAKES 1 ½ CUPS

Cheesy Potato Soup

4 potatoes, about 1–1½ pounds

2 tablespoons butter

1 medium onion, sliced

2 tablespoons all-purpose flour

1 teaspoon beef bouillon granules

2 cups water

1 (12-ounce) can evaporated milk

4 ounces **Widmer's Wisconsin Brick cheese,** shredded

1 teaspoon chopped parsley

¾ teaspoon Worcestershire sauce

¾ teaspoon black pepper

¾ teaspoon salt

Cook whole potatoes in microwave on high until tender, then cool.

Cook butter and onions in a large bowl in microwave on high until tender, about 2 minutes.

Stir in flour, then add bouillon granules and water before cooking in microwave again on high power for 2 minutes or until mixture is heated.

Scoop out potatoes, leaving pieces in chunks, then add to hot mixture along with evaporated milk, brick cheese, and seasonings.

Cook for 2–4 minutes in microwave until cheese is melted and soup is hot.

SERVES 6

Colby-Swiss Cheese Soup

1 pound fresh broccoli or 1 (10-ounce) bag frozen cut broccoli, thawed

½ cup water

1½ teaspoons instant chicken bouillon granules

2 medium carrots, thinly sliced

3 tablespoons butter

¼ cup sliced green onions

3 tablespoons all-purpose flour

½ teaspoon ground nutmeg

¼ teaspoon white pepper

3 cups milk

2 cups (8 ounces) shredded **Widmer's Colby cheese**

1 cup (4 ounces) shredded Wisconsin Swiss cheese

¼ cup dry sherry

If using fresh broccoli, remove outer leaves and tough parts of stalks. Cut stalks into bite-size pieces, about 4 cups.

Heat water and chicken bouillon granules in a large saucepan until boiling, then add carrots and broccoli. Cover and cook for 10 minutes or until vegetables are crisp-tender.

Drain, reserving the liquid, and set both vegetables and liquid aside.

Melt butter in a saucepan and add green onions, cooking until tender but not brown, then stir in flour, nutmeg, and white pepper. Add milk and reserved liquid all at once, stirring and cooking until thickened and bubbly. Cook and stir 1–2 minutes more.

Add cheeses and cook and stir until entirely melted. Stir in cooked vegetables and sherry and cook until heated through.

Top each serving with additional shredded Colby, if desired.

SERVES 6

Wisconsin Colby Cheese Scones

2 cups all-purpose flour

2 tablespoons sugar

1 tablespoon baking powder

½ teaspoon salt

¼ teaspoon baking soda

1¼ cup (5 ounces) shredded **Widmer's Colby cheese**

½ cup sour cream

3 tablespoons milk, plus more for brushing scones

1 egg, beaten

¼ cup oil

Preheat oven to 425°F.

In a large bowl, combine dry ingredients and cheese, then add sour cream mixed with milk, egg, and oil. Stir until mixture forms a ball.

Knead fifteen times on a floured surface. Divide dough into two 7-inch flat circles and brush tops with milk. Cut each circle of dough into eight wedges.

Place wedges 2 inches apart on a greased cookie sheet. Bake for 10–12 minutes or until bottoms are golden brown.

MAKES 16 SCONES

Wisconsin Cheese Scalloped Carrots

12 medium carrots, peeled and thinly sliced

½ cup (1 stick) butter, divided

1 medium onion, finely chopped

¼ cup all-purpose flour

¾ teaspoon salt

½ teaspoon dry mustard

2 cups milk

½ teaspoon ground white pepper

1 teaspoon celery seed

⅛ teaspoon cayenne pepper

2 cups (8 ounces) shredded **Widmer's sharp cheddar**

3 cups fresh bread crumbs

Preheat oven to 350°F. Lightly grease a 2-quart casserole dish.

Cook carrots in lightly salted water until barely tender, about 15 minutes, and drain.

Melt 4 tablespoons butter in a saucepan and sauté onions for 3 minutes. Stir in flour, salt, and mustard, and cook for 1 minute. Slowly stir in milk until smooth and thickened, adding white pepper, celery seed, and cayenne pepper.

Arrange one-third of carrots and cheese in baking dish, then pour one-third of sauce over it. Repeat until carrots, cheese, and sauce are all used.

Melt remaining 4 tablespoons butter. Stir in bread crumbs until coated and top casserole with crumb mixture.

Bake for 35–45 minutes or until bubbling and golden brown.

SERVES 8–12

Chili Cheese Rice

1 cup chopped onion

4 tablespoons butter

4 cups cooked rice

2 cups sour cream

1 cup cream-style cottage cheese

1 large bay leaf, crumbled

½ teaspoon salt

½ teaspoon black pepper

3 (4-ounce) cans green chiles, chopped

2 cups (16 ounces) shredded **Widmer's cheddar cheese**

Chopped parsley, for garnish

Preheat oven to 375°F. Lightly grease a 12 x 8-inch baking dish.

Sauté onion in butter until golden and remove from heat. Add hot rice, sour cream, cottage cheese, bay leaf, salt, and pepper. Mix well.

Layer half the rice mixture in baking dish, sprinkling chiles and half the cheese on top. Top with remaining rice and cheese and sprinkle parsley on top.

Bake for 25–30 minutes.

SERVES 8—10

Northwest Wisconsin

ANCHORING THE ARTISAN-CHEESE SLICE of this part of Wisconsin—where commodity cheeses are the bulk of production—is Marieke Penterman, who gave up her life in Holland to follow a dairy farmer to Thorp. They are now married and have five children. When she missed Gouda from her homeland, she decided to make it herself, surprising everyone when her Marieke Gouda earned Grand Champion at the US Championship Cheese Contest in 2013, just seven years after making her first batch. Visitors to Holland's Family Cheese can dine at Café Dutchess, get a glimpse at the creamery's operation, and participate in fun, family-friendly activities like story time in the barn (paired with grilled-cheese sandwiches).

Another entrepreneurial success story in Northwest Wisconsin is Ellsworth Cooperative Creamery, where owner Paul Bauer has been busy exporting cheese curds—after all, this community was dubbed Wisconsin's cheese-curd capital back in the 1980s by a former governor—to China. Every June a cheese-curd festival reminds locals of the village's most precious product. Bauer's also keeping this 108-year-old creamery alive, sourcing milk from four hundred family farms.

Turtle Lake is a small village with around one thousand residents. Resident cheesemaker Christophe Megevand crafts artisan cheese at Yellow Door Creamery, a boutique label under Italian-cheese importer Schuman Cheese. He relies on his nearly forty years of memories making cheese, starting in France, and uses antique methods like copper vats to craft small batches.

Burnett Dairy Cooperative

"IT'S KIND OF LIKE TAKING SCIENCE and being artistic with it," says Burnett Dairy Cooperative's Bruce Willis, a Master Cheesemaker, about the process of not only making but aging cheese, and developing a distinct flavor profile.

Although the first in his family to make cheese, he's no stranger to farm life. He worked on beef farms as a teen. "We sometimes worked until ten or eleven at night," he says. "They called me up when the calves were out to clean up the pens." After high school he joined the dairy cooperative, learning the science aspect of cheese, becoming its supervisor and cheesemaker two years later.

That was forty-five years ago.

"I didn't ever plan on staying here as long as I did," says Willis. "It was just a job to buy a car and all that." He quickly fell in love with cheese. "I got into it," he says, with a chuckle. "They call me the rookie even though I've been here forty-five years," he says, alluding to his first-generation cheesemaker status.

Willis has witnessed many changes in the dairy industry over the last four decades. "There were probably 260-some farms at one time, for this co-op, back in the 1980s," he says. Large companies bought up the smaller farms. Today the cooperative—which sells cheese under the Cady Creek Farms, Burnett Dairy, and Wood River Creamery labels—sources milk from around two hundred different dairies and is owned by farmers.

Dating back to 1896, one of the three founding creameries (originally called Wood Lake Creamery) is honored today in one of the cooperative's brands as Wood River Creamery. In the 1960s those three creameries merged into one—two later closed.

At home, Willis turns to his own cheeses when tinkering in the kitchen. He's not so much a fan of recipes as he is playing around with flavors. "I like to use Wood River Creamery with Black Summer Truffle, an Alpine-style cheddar, in macaroni and cheese. I blend it with the other cheeses," he says. Wood River Creamery with Applewood Smoked Sea Salt is another one of his favorites: "That's real good with cheeseburgers," he says. Another perennial choice at home is the Wood River Creamery with Herbes de Provence—with chicken dishes.

Cornmeal-Crusted Fish Tacos

1 pound white-fleshed fish (such as cod, haddock, tilapia, or halibut), cut into 2- by 1-inch pieces

¾ teaspoon salt, divided

½ teaspoon freshly ground black pepper, divided

⅓ cup cornmeal

¼ cup canola oil

½ cup sour cream

½ teaspoon finely grated lime zest

1 tablespoon lime juice

¼ teaspoon ground cumin

8 (7-inch) corn or flour tortillas, warmed

2 cups shredded Bibb lettuce or red cabbage

½ cup prepared tomatillo salsa

1 cup (8 ounces) shredded **Wood River Creamery Mango Habanero Alpine-Style Cheddar Cheese**

¼ cup finely chopped red onion

Season fish with ½ teaspoon salt and ¼ teaspoon pepper, then dredge in cornmeal. In a large nonstick skillet, cook fish in oil over medium heat for 2–4 minutes per side or until lightly golden and cooked through. Transfer to a plate lined with paper towels.

Stir together sour cream, lime zest, lime juice, cumin, and remaining salt and pepper. Assemble fish in tortillas with lettuce or cabbage, salsa, cheese, and red onion. Drizzle with sour cream mixture.

For fully loaded tacos, add avocado, cucumber, and fresh cilantro.

Serves 4

Ultimate Grilled-Cheese Breakfast Sandwich

8 slices peameal bacon, cooked

2 tablespoons olive oil

4 eggs, pan-fried

2 tablespoons butter, room temperature

8 slices sourdough bread

3 tablespoons grainy mustard

8 ounces **Wood River Original Alpine-Style Cheddar,** cut into 8 slices

To cook peameal bacon, blot with a paper towel. Cook in a large nonstick skillet over medium heat for 3–5 minutes per side or until browned. Transfer to a plate.

To pan-fry eggs, heat olive oil in a skillet over medium heat. Crack eggs into skillet, then cover and cook for 2–4 minutes or until whites are set and yolks are soft but not runny, or until desired doneness.

Butter one side of each bread slice. Spread grainy mustard on unbuttered sides of four of the bread slices. Place two slices of peameal bacon on top of mustard. Layer a cheese slice, fried egg, and another cheese slice over bacon. Cap with remaining slices of bread, buttered sides out.

Toast sandwiches in large nonstick skillet over medium-low heat for 2–3 minutes per side or until bread is golden and toasted and cheese is melted.

Serves 4

Canoe Bay

W16065 Hogback Rd.

Chetek

(715) 924-4594

canoebay.com

In 1993 this Chicago couple gave up high-profile careers (and high stress) in Chicago for a quieter lifestyle and deeper connection with the land.

Dan Dobrowolski grew up across the lake from the former Boy Scouts camp that he and his wife, Lisa, snapped up when it came up for sale. What used to mean lazy summers for kids is now one of the Midwest's poshest, most food- and design-intense destinations, set on three hundred luxurious acres.

Guests at Canoe Bay are treated to farm-to-table and in-season meals with ingredients so fresh it's a wonder they make it to this far-off spot in the woods. The vegetables, cheeses, and meats are easy, given Wisconsin's abundant farms and creameries, but the lobster? Not so much. Those are flown in to Minneapolis-St. Paul's airport and retrieved by kitchen staff in a four-hour round-trip trek by car. Most produce is procured on-site, in a three-acre garden tended to by John Nissen. Executive chef Randall Prudden, former sous chef at the esteemed Next Restaurant in Chicago, is in charge of the kitchen.

Another nod to Wisconsin's artisan bent: Some of the cabins and cottages were designed by John Rattenbury, a protégé of Frank Lloyd Wright. That same organic style of architecture where structures blend seamlessly into the natural surroundings, combined with the compressed entryways, blonde woods, and use of earth tones, is the perfect backdrop for showcasing Wisconsin's home-grown food. That includes cheese.

Many of the dishes served at dinner each night in the lodge's glass-walled dining room weave in Wisconsin cheese. This includes a grilled asparagus salad (when in season) featuring fresh sheep's milk cheese.

Despite the gourmet cuisine, there's a keen focus on re-creating the casual summer-camp experience. On one trip my husband and I were startled to see, on our canoe ride across the lake, a deer on the shoreline, gazing right at us. But for a few ripples in the lake and a cool gentle breeze, time stood still.

Ellsworth Cooperative Creamery

PAUL BAUER IS ON A MISSION to take cheese curds global.

This includes frying up his white cheddar cheese curds in beer batter in front of crowds in China, along with other members of the Ellsworth Cooperative Creamery. Their cheese has been exported here since 2013 and per-capita cheese consumption is climbing. "We started to go to the trade shows and people did not know what (cheese curds) are," says Bauer, CEO/manager of Ellsworth Cooperative Creamery. "They want to mimic what we can do. They don't really like pre-pared foods in China.

"I call myself an 'ag nerd.' I grew up on a dairy farm outside of Wausau," says Bauer, who runs the creamery's day-to-day oper-ations. Armed with an agricultural-business degree from UW–River Falls earned in the late '80s, he worked for Kraft, helped start two creameries (Antigo Cheese Company in Wisconsin and Blackfoot Cheese Company in Idaho), and then worked for Burnett Dairy Cooperative.

Snug in the heart of Wisconsin's cheese-curd capital, based on Gov. Anthony Earl's 1983 proclamation, the Ellsworth Cheese Curd Festival happens every June in this village 50 miles southeast of Minneapolis. It draws thousands of people to this small village. Entrants compete in a competitive curd-eating contest where the winner receives a com-memorative wall plaque, cash prize, and bragging rights.

Although the cooperative dates back 108 years, cheese production only began in 1968, with cheddar block and cheddar curds. Now 80 different varieties of specialty cheeses are made. Three plants make the cooperative's cheese: curds in Ellsworth, small-batch artisan cheese (including Muenster) in Comstock and cheese blends for the restau-rant industry in New London (acquired in 2018). They are sold under the labels Antonella, Blaser's, Ellsworth Cooperative Creamery, Kammerude and Ellsworth Valley. About 350 different family farms supply the milk, including families who have shipped milk to the cooperative for 108 years.

Caramel Apple Cheese Curds

5 filo sheets

½ cup (1 stick) butter, melted

½ cup cinnamon sugar, divided

2 quarts vegetable oil, for frying

2½ cups Granny Smith apples, diced into ¼-inch-thick pieces

2 tablespoons clarified butter

4 ounces hard cider

1½ cups pancake mix

½ cup all-purpose flour

1 egg

12 ounces light beer or hard apple cider

1 cup cornstarch, for dredging

1 pound **Ellsworth Cooperative Creamery Natural Cheese Curds**

MAPLE BOURBON CARAMEL SAUCE:

1 cup firmly packed brown sugar

½ cup (1 stick) butter

¼ cup half-and-half

¼ cup maple syrup

¼ cup bourbon

1 teaspoon balsamic vinegar

GARNISH:

Whipped cream, caramel sauce, sliced apples, and fresh mint

Preheat oven to 400°F.

Brush melted butter between each filo sheet, then dust top layer with cinnamon sugar. Cut into 3- by 3-inch squares and bake on a sheet pan until golden brown. Remove from oven and cool.

In a 4-quart saucepan, heat 2 quarts oil to 350–360°F.

Prepare apple compote by sautéing apples in clarified butter. Simmer on medium heat with hard cider and 1 tablespoon cinnamon sugar until most of the liquid has reduced and apples are soft.

To make batter for the cheese curds, mix pancake mix, flour, egg, and beer in a bowl. Whisk until smooth and thin. Place cornstarch in a large, shallow dish.

Dip cheese curds eight at a time into cornstarch, shake off excess, and drop into batter. Shaking off excess batter, gently place into hot oil. Fry until golden brown, then move with a strainer to a bowl and toss with 1 tablespoon cinnamon sugar. Repeat process until all cheese curds have been fried and dusted with cinnamon sugar.

FOR MAPLE BOURBON CARAMEL SAUCE:

Heat brown sugar and butter over medium-high heat in a large saucepan, stirring with a wooden spoon until sugar is dissolved. Bring to a boil with half-and-half, maple syrup, bourbon, and balsamic vinegar, stirring for 3–4 minutes until smooth and thick.

Serve warm or at room temperature. Refrigerate remaining sauce in a screw-top jar for up to a month.

TO ASSEMBLE:

Put one baked filo square in center of a plate and top with ¼ cup warm apple filling and three or four fried cheese curds. Top with an additional baked filo square and garnish with vanilla whipped cream, caramel sauce, thinly sliced apples, and a sprig of fresh mint.

SERVES 8

Cheese Curd and Jalapeño Drop Biscuits

2 cups all-purpose flour

2 teaspoons baking powder

½ teaspoon baking soda

1 tablespoon sugar

½ teaspoon kosher salt

Pinch of cayenne pepper

6 tablespoons unsalted butter, frozen

3 tablespoons finely diced roasted jalapeños

8 ounces **Ellsworth Cooperative Creamery Natural Cheese Curd Crumbles**

1⅓ cups buttermilk

Preheat oven to 425°F. Grease a large baking sheet.

Whisk together flour, baking powder, baking soda, sugar, salt, and cayenne pepper.

Grate frozen butter using a cheese grater. Using a pastry knife or fork, cut in butter to incorporate with dry mixture and fold in jalapeños and cheese curd crumbles.

Stir in buttermilk but do not overmix.

Using a 2-ounce scoop, drop dough onto prepared baking sheet.

Bake for 15 minutes or until lightly browned.

MAKES 15 BISCUITS

Chicken Cordon New

1 skinless, boneless breast of chicken

Salt and pepper, to taste

2 tablespoons olive oil, divided

¼ cup julienned onion

1 cup baby arugula

2 ounces **Ellsworth Cooperative Creamery Cheese Curd Crumbles**

3 slices thin prosciutto

Slice chicken breast lengthwise, creating two even cutlets. Season with salt and pepper and sear in a pre-heated sauté pan using 1 tablespoon olive oil. Brown on both sides and remove from pan.

In the same pan caramelize julienned onion in remaining 1 tablespoon olive oil and gently wilt arugula. Remove from pan to cool.

Place cooked breasts on a cutting board and top with wilted arugula and caramelized onion, plus a small amount of cheese curd crumbles and remaining chicken cutlet.

Place stuffed chicken breast on three slices prosciutto and roll up tightly.

Preheat oven to 400°F.

Spread remaining cheese curd crumbles on a non-stick sheet pan to form a 3½- by 5-inch rectangle. Bake for 5–7 minutes until cheese has melted and is golden brown.

Place wrapped chicken breast on top of cheese and roll up tightly. Return to oven to crisp up cheese and warm through. Chicken should reach an internal temperature of 165°F. Remove from oven.

Garnish with seasonal vegetables and a drizzle of olive oil and balsamic vinegar.

SERVES 1

The Lakely

Inside Oxbow Hotel
516 Galloway St.
Eau Claire
(715) 839-0601
thelakely.com

It's not every day a Grammy Award–winning musician opens a boutique hotel in his hometown.

That's exactly what Justin Vernon (of indie folk band Bon Iver, which won Best New Artist at the 2012 Grammys) did in late 2016 when he opened Oxbow Hotel in downtown Eau Claire with Zach Halmstad and Nick Meyer. His hit songs include "Skinny Love," off Bon Iver's debut album *For Emma, Forever Ago*, released in 2007.

Having risen to fame after recording that album in a North Woods cabin during a brutal winter, this is Vernon's personal homage to the community that has supported him. In addition to the hotel, he hosts and organizes a music festival in this northern Wisconsin city each July called Eaux Claires.

At The Lakely, live jazz and Midwestern takes on comfort food are what draw people in. Chef Nathan Berg's number-one focus is helping to develop a distinct Upper Midwest style of cuisine, which is reflected in dishes like the Koldtbord, what the Danish call their Swedish version of smorgasbord. On it are artisan meats, cheeses, chopped raw vegetables, crackers, and more. Diners check off the items they want and *voilà*! It's served to the table.

From start to finish, nearly the entire meal is locally sourced, from a Rushing Waters smoked-trout salad to pan-seared Bell & Evans chicken served with native-harvested wild rice and culminating with a glass of Wollersheim Port paired with the seasonally derived dessert. (If it's summer, order the lavender shortcake with market strawberries with Vikre Distillery's cedar-gin syrup.) Wisconsin cheese is sprinkled throughout the menu, in line with the farm-to-table mission, whether it's Sartori's SarVecchio in spring risotto or Hook's cheddar on top of a burger.

Holland's Family Cheese

THE SHORT VERSION OF THE STORY is that Marieke Penterman followed a cute guy from Holland to Wisconsin.

But after becoming a mom and supporting her husband, Rolf, on his dairy farm, she yearned for her own career.

"I really wanted to start something for myself," she says, after the first two of her five children were born. "I wanted to do something before I turned fifty. One night I tossed and turned and I heard a cow calving." She decided to make cheese.

Her reasons were also selfish: This Netherlands native missed Gouda. "I couldn't get used to Colby and cheddar (in Wisconsin)," she says. An internship at the former Dairy Business Innovation Center was followed by an internship with a cheesemaker. "Before we started this crazy adventure, I'd never made cheese in my whole life," she says.

In November 2006 she released her first batch of Marieke Gouda. Four months later she won her first award, which included attending a banquet where she knew no one. One cheesemaker remarked to her that he'd been making cheese for twenty years and never won an award.

Then in 2013 Marieke Gouda Mature (6–9 Months) was named Grand Champion of the US Championship Cheese Contest. This made her eligible for a green card through extraordinary-ability status. "Normally that's for athletes and professors," says Penterman, who believes in supporting other female cheesemakers. Three women make cheese at Marieke Gouda. One has been there for eleven years.

The Thorp farmstead includes Café Dutchess (open for breakfast and lunch), a glass-walled creamery (so visitors can witness the process of making cheese), and family-friendly activities each summer like Book in the Barn (grilled-cheese lunch with book reading on hay bales).

Will her children be the creamery's next generation? "I'd rather have them put their feet under someone else's table for a while," she says. Her two oldest—fifteen-year-old twins—plan to work at local grocery and hardware stores for their first part-time jobs. "They can always come back."

But for now the family enjoys Saturday brunch—made by the kids. "It's a Penterman tradition. Every Saturday morning, they get up and make the ham and cheese croissants," she says, the perfect start to Rolf's day off.

Other ways the Pentermans eat their Gouda at home include mushrooms stuffed with cream cheese and topped with Gouda, carbonara with bacon and heavy cream topped with grated Gouda, and simply Gouda with mustard. "I like to enjoy the Gouda cheese with an imported mustard from Holland and have a cold beer," says Penterman.

Flavorful Marieke Gouda Burgers

2 pounds ground beef

1 tablespoon Worcestershire sauce

2 tablespoons barbecue sauce

1 teaspoon steak seasoning

½ cup plus 6 tablespoons shredded **Marieke Gouda Black Pepper Mix**

6 large hamburger buns

Burger sauce: ¼ cup ketchup, ¼ cup mayonnaise, and 1 garlic clove (pressed)

Gently toss with a fork to combine ground beef, Worcestershire sauce, barbecue sauce, steak seasoning, and ½ cup Marieke Gouda Black Pepper Mix.

Shape beef into six patties. Grill until burgers reach an internal temperature of 130°F. Top each burger with 1 tablespoon Marieke Gouda Black Pepper Mix. Cook until cheese is melted, about 1 minute.

Transfer burgers to a plate. Let rest for 5 minutes.

Toast hamburger buns cut-side down in a skillet with butter until golden brown.

Whisk all ingredients for burger sauce in a small bowl.

Transfer burgers to toasted buns and top with burger sauce. Serve immediately.

Recipe by Molly Schraufnagel

SERVES 6

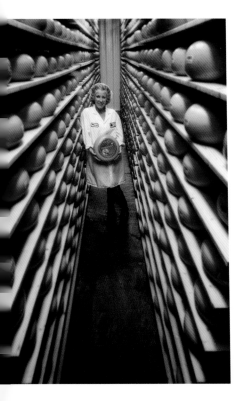

Grilled Marieke Gouda Potato Skins

4 medium russet potatoes, scrubbed

2 tablespoons extra-virgin olive oil

1 garlic clove, minced

½ teaspoon salt

¼ teaspoon black pepper

1 cup finely shredded **Marieke Gouda Onion Garlic**

2 slices cooked bacon, crumbled

1-2 tablespoons snipped fresh chives

Sour cream

Preheat grill to medium-heat.

Cut each potato into quarters, lengthwise. Place on a microwave-safe plate and cook on high for 5-6 minutes or until potatoes start to get tender.

Cut away flesh of potato leaving a ¼-inch shell.

Microwave olive oil and garlic, combined, for 1 minute. Brush both sides of each potato skin with olive oil and garlic mixture. Season with salt and pepper.

Grill potato skins 4-5 minutes on each side until crisp. Remove from grill and place on a cookie sheet.

Top each potato skin with a teaspoon of Marieke Gouda Onion Garlic. Place back on the grill long enough for cheese to melt.

Top potato skins with crumbled bacon, chives, and sour cream.

Recipe by Molly Schraufnagel

SERVES 4

Foenegreek Gouda Grilled French Toast

1½ cups half-and-half, warmed

2 large eggs

2 tablespoons brown sugar

¾ teaspoon cinnamon

2 tablespoons butter, melted

2 teaspoons vanilla

8 slices hearty white bread

1 pound bacon, cooked

6 ounces **Marieke Foenegreek Gouda,** shredded

2–3 tablespoons butter, softened

Heat a large skillet over medium-heat. Coat with cooking spray.

Whisk half-and-half, eggs, brown sugar, cinnamon, butter, and vanilla in a medium bowl. Transfer to a large, shallow dish.

Soak each slice of bread in egg mixture and then cook until golden brown, 4–5 minutes. Flip and continue to cook until both sides are golden brown.

On a clean work surface, place bacon on four slices of french toast and top each with one-quarter of the cheese.

Top with another slice of french toast and press down gently to set. Spread sandwich tops with half the softened butter.

Place sandwiches buttered side down in the skillet and spread the other side of each sandwich with remaining butter. Cook until crisp and golden brown, when cheese starts to melt. Flip and continue cooking until cheese completely melts.

Serve immediately with your favorite syrup.

Recipe by Molly Schraufnagel

SERVES 4

Ultimate Marieke Gouda Smoked Nachos

¼ fresh pineapple, peeled

1 tablespoon vegetable oil

1 garlic clove, pressed

½ teaspoon chili powder

2 tablespoons finely chopped onion

1 cup ketchup

½ cup brown sugar

2 cups shredded cooked chicken

8 ounces tortilla chips

2 cups shredded **Marieke Gouda Smoked**

1 cup shredded **Marieke Gouda Plain Young**

2 green onions, thinly sliced

1 avocado, cut into small chunks

Preheat grill.

Cut pineapple crosswise into ½-inch-thick slices. Place on grill over medium heat. Grill pineapple on each side until lightly charred. Let cool. Slice into ¼-inch pieces and set aside.

Adjust oven rack to middle position and preheat oven to 400°F.

In a medium-size saucepan, heat oil and add garlic and chili powder, stirring until fragrant. Continue stirring and add onions. Cook for 1 minute. Add ketchup and brown sugar. Simmer for 5–7 minutes, stirring frequently.

Add chicken to sauce. Continue to simmer while preparing pan of nachos.

Spread chips in an even layer in an 11 x 15-inch baking pan. Sprinkle chips evenly with chicken mixture, pineapple pieces, and Marieke Gouda Smoked and Plain Young cheeses. Bake until cheese is melted, 5–7 minutes.

Remove nachos from oven and sprinkle with green onions and avocados.

Serve immediately.

Recipe by Molly Schraufnagel

SERVES 6

Yellow Door Creamery

THE COUNTRY'S LARGEST IMPORTER of Italian cheese (Schuman Cheese) has two artisan-cheese lines in Wisconsin.

French Alps native Christophe Megevand serves as head cheesemaker at Montforte Dairy in Montforte (blue cheese and Gorgonzola) and Yellow Door Creamery in Turtle Lake (Fontina and Alpine styles).

His "off-the-beaten path" approach at Yellow Door Creamery means using copper vats (a technique employed by few American cheesemakers). "By having access to a copper vat, we extended the line into smaller batches of Alpine (style) cheese," says Megevand. The cheesemakers traveled to France, for an in-depth tutorial in old-world techniques in making cheese, as part of an exchange with students from France who traveled to the United States to learn about Wisconsin cheesemaking at Yellow Door Creamery.

"We are very close to traditional cheesemaking in the Alps of France," Megevand says, pointing to Wisconsin's *terroir* (French for soil's sense of place or, in creamery terms, "a tie between the land, the feed, and the cows," he says) as the main reason. "It's a lake region with lots of forests and agricultural land." The majority of cow's milk is sourced from within fifty miles of the creamery. "We know how they feed and take care of the animals," he says. "The relationship they have with us is very personal and unique."

The cheeses, five hand-rubbed fontinas—Tuscan, Bergamot & Hibiscus, Mayan Cocoa & Coffee, Dijon Herb, and Harissa—and three Alpine-style varieties—Valis, Monteau, and Altu—are cured and aged for up to 180 days on-site.

Within the last three years, all of Yellow Door Creamery's cheeses have taken top honors at the US Championship Cheese Contest, World Championship Cheese Contest, and International Cheese Awards.

Tuscan Tomato Frittata

2 tablespoons olive oil

1 shallot, finely diced

2 garlic cloves, minced

8 large eggs

½ cup heavy cream

1 wedge **Yellow Door Creamery Tuscan Rubbed Fontina,** shredded

1 pint cherry tomatoes, halved

2 tablespoons chopped mixed fresh herbs (tarragon, rosemary, thyme, oregano, parsley, and chives)

Salt and pepper, to taste

Preheat oven to 400°F.

Heat the olive oil in a large, oven-safe skillet over medium heat. Add the shallot and garlic and sauté until the veggies are fragrant and translucent, around 5 minutes.

In the meantime, add the eggs, cream, and shredded fontina to a medium-size bowl. Whisk until the eggs are well beaten and fluffy and pour over the sautéed shallot and garlic. Let the frittata cook for a few minutes over medium heat, just until set on the bottom.

Top the frittata with the halved cherry tomatoes and bake for 10–15 minutes or until cooked through and set in the middle.

Let the frittata cool slightly, top with herbs, season with salt and pepper to taste and serve.

SERVES 8

Zucchini and Fontina Fritters with Lemon Aioli

LEMON AIOLI:

1 cup Vegenaise

2 teaspoons granulated garlic

1 teaspoon lemon zest

1 tablespoon lemon juice

2 tablespoons agave or honey

FRITTERS:

2 tablespoons olive oil

2 small zucchini, shredded

2 scallions, thinly diced

1 large egg

¼ cup all-purpose flour

¾ cup shredded **Yellow Door Tuscan Rubbed Fontina**

1 teaspoon salt

FOR LEMON AIOLI:

Whisk all ingredients together and set aside.

FOR FRITTERS:

Heat the olive oil in a large nonstick skillet or griddle over medium heat.

Place the shredded zucchini in a clean dish towel or a cheesecloth and squeeze out all the water over the sink. Don't skip this step or you'll end up with soggy fritters.

Once the zucchini has been squeezed dry, transfer to a large mixing bowl and add scallions, egg, flour, cheese, and salt. Mix to combine.

Scoop ¼ cup batter for each fritter and pour into the hot oil. Depending on how big your pan is, you can cook anywhere between two and six fritters at a time. Fry the fritters for 1-2 minutes on each side or until golden brown and crispy around the edges. Serve with lemon aioli.

SERVES 4

Baked Gnocchi with Pumpkin and Fontina

2 tablespoons butter, melted

½ cup milk

1½ cups pure pumpkin puree

1 (16-ounce) package fresh gnocchi

1 wedge **Yellow Door Creamery Tuscan Rubbed Fontina,** shredded

4 tablespoons chopped mixed fresh herbs (tarragon, rosemary, thyme, oregano), divided

½ teaspoon crushed red pepper

Salt and pepper, to taste

Preheat oven to 350°F. Lightly grease a large casserole dish.

Whisk the butter, milk, crushed red pepper, pumpkin puree, salt, and pepper in a large bowl. Mix in the gnocchi, 3 tablespoons fresh herbs, and half the shredded cheese, reserving the second half to sprinkle on top.

Pour the gnocchi mixture in prepared casserole dish and sprinkle on the remaining shredded fontina cheese and fresh herbs. Bake for 20–25 minutes or until the gnocchi are fork-tender and the cheese is melted and golden brown on top.

SERVES 8

Tuscan Fontina Salad

CHAMPAGNE VINAIGRETTE:

3 tablespoons extra-virgin olive oil

3 tablespoons champagne vinegar

1 tablespoons whole-grain mustard

3 tablespoons honey

Salt and pepper, to taste

5 ounces baby arugula

1 cup slow-roasted oven tomatoes

1 wedge **Yellow Door Creamery Tuscan Rubbed Fontina,** cubed

½ cup toasted pine nuts

2 ounces micro basil

1 bunch roasted asparagus

3 whole green onions, halved lengthwise

FOR CHAMPAGNE VINAIGRETTE:

Whisk olive oil, vinegar, mustard, honey, and salt and pepper in a small bowl. Set aside.

FOR SALAD:

Top arugula with tomatoes, fontina, and pine nuts, then toss with champagne vinaigrette. Top with micro basil. Serve with roasted asparagus and halved green onions.

Recipe by Allison Schuman, Schuman Cheese Director of Sales

SERVES 6

Mediterranean Quiche

1 (10-inch) pie crust

2 tablespoons olive oil

½ cup diced red onion

½ cup fresh baby spinach

⅛ cup diced red bell pepper

3 large eggs

¾ cup heavy cream

1 teaspoon sea salt

1 teaspoon cracked black pepper

1 cup shredded **Yellow Door Creamery Tuscan Rubbed Fontina**

⅛ cup diced canned artichoke hearts

⅛ cup diced kalamata olives

Preheat oven to 375°F.

Follow package instructions to bake one 10-inch pie crust. Before baking, cover with a double layer of heavy-duty aluminum foil. Place pie weights or dried beans on top. Bake until edges are lightly browned. Allow to cool while you prepare the filling.

In a sauté pan over medium heat, add olive oil, onions, spinach, and red pepper. Sauté and stir until the onions are translucent and spinach is cooked, about 5 minutes. Set pan aside to cool slightly.

In a large bowl, whisk the eggs. Add the heavy cream, sea salt, and cracked black pepper and whisk until well combined. Gently stir in the shredded Yellow Door Creamery Tuscan Rubbed Fontina, then the cooled vegetable mixture, artichokes, and the olives.

Pour filling into the pre-baked crust and bake until the custard is set, about 45–60 minutes.

Remove from oven and allow to cool for 10 minutes before cutting.

SERVES 4

Mushroom Fontina Tart

1 sheet frozen puff pastry

All-purpose flour, for dusting

1 egg, beaten

½ cup shredded **Yellow Door Creamery Tuscan Rubbed Fontina**

MUSHROOM SAUTÉ:

2 tablespoons olive oil

1 pound mixed fresh mushrooms, sliced ¼ inch thick, to yield 5½–6 cups

2 garlic cloves, minced

½ teaspoon sea salt

Freshly ground black pepper

Additional chopped herbs, such as thyme, sage, and/or chives, optional

BLISTERED CHERRY TOMATOES:

2 pints cherry tomatoes

1 tablespoon olive oil

Sea salt

Thaw one sheet of frozen puff pastry at room temperature until pliable, 30–45 minutes.

FOR MUSHROOM SAUTÉ:

Heat the oil in a 12-inch sauté pan or skillet over medium heat. Add the mushrooms and garlic, sprinkle with the salt, and stir for 2–3 minutes. Increase the heat to medium-high so that you hear a steady sizzle; stir occasionally for approximately 5 minutes until browned. Stir in pepper and fresh herbs. Set the sauté aside to cool.

FOR BLISTERED CHERRY TOMATOES:

Using your heaviest cast-iron skillet, heat the oil over medium-high heat, add the cherry tomatoes, and let sit for 2 minutes until they start to blister. Quickly stir and blister to desired amount of color and sprinkle with salt.

FOR TART:

Center rack in oven and preheat to 425°F.

Lightly dust a work surface with flour. Unfold the pastry sheet and roll it into a rectangle about 10 by 15 inches and about ¹⁄₁₆ inch thick. Slide it onto a baking sheet lined with parchment. With the exception of about an inch border around the rectangle, prick the pastry all over with a fork. Brush the beaten egg over the border.

Bake until the pastry begins to puff and the surface feels dry, about 5 minutes.

Top pastry with shredded Yellow Door Creamery Tuscan Rubbed Fontina, leaving an inch or so border. Scatter mushroom sauté and blistered cherry tomatoes over the crust. Bake until the crust border is puffed and deeply golden brown, about 10 minutes.

Let cool briefly. Top with more fresh herbs.

SERVES 12

Tuscan Mac-n-Cheese

1 head garlic

1–2 teaspoons olive oil

2 tablespoons butter

2 tablespoons all-purpose flour

2 cups warm milk

1 teaspoon sea salt

1 teaspoon cracked black pepper

3 cups shredded **Yellow Door Creamery Tuscan Rubbed Fontina,** divided

1 cup baby spinach

1 (16-ounce) package conchiglie (small sea shell) pasta, cooked

Preheat oven to 400°F.

Trim about ¼ inch off the top of the head of garlic to expose tops of cloves. Drizzle with 1–2 teaspoons olive oil and roast for 30–40 minutes or until caramelized. When cool, pull or squeeze roasted garlic from skins and set aside.

Melt butter in a large skillet or Dutch oven over medium-low heat; whisk in flour until smooth. Cook, whisking constantly, for 1 minute. Gradually whisk in warm milk and cook, whisking constantly, for 5 minutes or until thickened.

Whisk in sea salt, cracked black pepper, 2 cups shredded Yellow Door Creamery Tuscan Rubbed Fontina, baby spinach, and roasted garlic, then stir in pasta.

Spoon pasta mixture into a lightly greased 3-quart baking dish and top with remaining Tuscan Rubbed Fontina.

Bake at 400°F for 20 minutes or until golden and bubbly.

SERVES 8

Tuscan Penne Pasta

SLOW-ROASTED TOMATOES:

1¼ pounds cherry tomatoes

Splash of olive oil

Sea salt and cracked black pepper

PASTA:

1 (16-ounce) package penne pasta, cooked

2 tablespoons chopped fresh oregano

2 tablespoons chopped fresh thyme

2 tablespoons chopped fresh basil

2 tablespoons chopped fresh parsley

2 tablespoons Meyer lemon zest

¼ cup capers

¼ cup olive oil

Juice from 1 Meyer lemon

1 teaspoon sea salt

1 teaspoon cracked black pepper

2 cups shredded **Yellow Door Tuscan Rubbed Fontina**

FOR SLOW-ROASTED TOMATOES:

Preheat oven to 325°F.

Place tomatoes on a rimmed baking sheet. Drizzle with olive oil and sprinkle with sea salt and cracked black pepper.

Roast until tomatoes begin to collapse, about 90 minutes.

FOR PASTA:

Cook penne pasta according to package directions and cool slightly.

In a large bowl, combine pasta, fresh herbs, lemon zest, capers, slow-roasted cherry tomatoes, olive oil, lemon juice, sea salt, and cracked black pepper; toss together.

Gently mix in the shredded Yellow Door Creamery Tuscan Rubbed Fontina.

SERVES 8

Appendix A
Cheese Award Winners

Southwest Wisconsin

Bleu Mont Dairy

3rd place in 2017 American Cheese Society's Judging & Competition's "Cheddar Wrapped in Cloth, Linen, Aged Over 12 Months, All Milks" category: "Reserve" Bandaged Cheddar

3rd place in 2017 American Cheese Society's Judging & Competition's "Cheddar Wrapped in Cloth, Linen, Aged up to 12 Months, All Milks" category: Bandaged Cheddar

Carr Valley Cheese

1st place in 2017 US Championship Cheese Contest's "Prepared Cheese Foods" category: Garlic Bread Cheese

2nd place in 2017 US Championship Cheese Contest's "Soft & Semi-Soft Mixed Milk Cheeses" category: Mobay

2nd place in 2017 US Championship Cheese Contest's "Flavored Semi-Soft Goat's Milk Cheeses" category: Cocoa Cardona

2nd place in 2017 US Championship Cheese Contest's "Hard Goat's Milk Cheeses" category: Cave Aged Cardona

1st place in 2017 US Championship Cheese Contest's "Cold Pack Cheese Spreads" category: Swiss Almond Cold Pack Spread

2nd place in 2017 US Championship Cheese Contest's "Open Class: Pepper Flavored Cheese, Medium Heat" category: Cranberry Chipotle Cheddar

1st place in 2018 World Championship Cheese Contest's "Prepared Cheese" category: Chipotle Bread Cheese

2nd place in 2018 World Championship Cheese Contest's "Surface (Mold) Ripened Mixed Milk Cheeses" category: Cave Aged Melange

2nd place in 2018 World Championship Cheese Contest's "Surface (Mold) Ripened Goat's Milk Cheeses" category: Snow White Goat Cheddar

2nd place in 2018 World Championship Cheese Contest's "Flavored Semi-Soft (Semi-Hard) Goat's Milk Cheese" category: Black Goat Truffle

2nd place in 2018 World Championship Cheese Contest's "Flavored Semi-Soft (Semi-Hard) Goat's Milk Cheese" category: Cocoa Cardona

Cedar Grove Cheese

1st place in 2017 American Cheese Society's Judging & Competition's "Open Category: Washed Rind Cheeses Aged More than 60 days, Up to 42% moisture, Made from Sheep's Milk" category: Cestino Pecora

1st place in 2017 American Cheese Society's Judging & Competition's "American Originals Original Recipe/Open Category, Made from Mixed or Other Milks" category: Montague

1st place in 2017 American Cheese Society's Judging & Competition's "American Originals Original Recipe/Open Category, Made from Cow's Milk" category: Ovella

3rd place in 2017 US Championship Cheese Contest's "Hard Sheep's Milk Cheese" category: Donatello

Crave Brothers Farmstead Cheese

1st place in 2017 American Cheese Society's Judging & Competition's "Fresh Mozzarella—Under 8 oz. (Ovalini, Bocconcini, Ciliegine sizes), All Milks" category: Fresh Mozzarella, Under 8 ounces

2nd place in 2017 American Cheese Society's Judging & Competition's "Fresh Mozzarella—8 oz. or More (Balls or Shapes), All Milks" category: Fresh Mozzarella

1st place in 2017 US Championship Cheese Contest's "Natural Snack Cheese" category: Jalapeno Cheddar Cheese Curds

1st place, 2nd place and 3rd place in 2017 US Championship Cheese Contest's "Fresh Mozzarella" category: Fresh Mozzarella

3rd place in 2018 World Championship Cheese Contest's "Fresh Mozzarella" category: Fresh Mozzarella

1st place in 2018 World Championship Cheese Contest's "Open Class: Flavored Soft Cheeses" category: Marinated Fresh Mozzarella

Edelweiss Creamery

2nd place in 2017 American Cheese Society's Judging & Competition's "International Style with Flavor Added, All Milks" category: Pepper Muenster

1st place in 2017 American Cheese Society's Judging & Competition's "Emmental-style with Eye Formation (Swiss, Baby Swiss, Blocks, Wheels), Made from Cow's Milk" category: Emmental

3rd place in 2017 American Cheese Society's Judging & Competition's "Brick Muenster, Made from Cow's Milk" category: Muenster

2nd place in 2017 American Cheese Society's Judging & Competition's "Brick Cheese, Made from Cow's Milk" category: Brick

3rd place in 2017 US Championship Cheese Contest's "Havarti" category: Havarti

1st place in 2018 World Championship Cheese Contest's "Havarti" category: Havarti

2nd place in 2018 World Championship Cheese Contest's "Havarti, Flavored" category: Havarti Onion

Emmi Roth

1st place in 2017 American Cheese Society's Judging & Competition's "Open Category: Washed Rind Cheeses Aged More than 60 days, Up to 42% moisture, Cow's Milk" category: Organic Grand Cru Reserve

3rd place in 2017 American Cheese Society's Judging & Competition's "Hispanic & Portuguese Style Cheeses: Ripened, Aged Over 90 days, All Milks" category: GranQueso

1st place in 2017 American Cheese Society's Judging & Competition's "American Originals Original Recipe/Open Category, Made from Cow's Milk" category: Roth's Private Reserve

1st place in 2017 US Championship Cheese Contest's "Open Class: Smear Ripened Hard Cheeses" category: Roth Grand Cru Reserve

2nd place in 2017 US Championship Cheese Contest's "Open Class: Smear Ripened Hard Cheeses" category: Roth's Private Reserve

3rd place in 2017 US Championship Cheese Contest's "Open Class: Smear Ripened Hard Cheeses" category: Roth Grand Cru Original

2nd place in 2017 US Championship Cheese Contest's "Blue Veined Cheeses" category: Roth Buttermilk Blue

1st place in 2017 US Championship Cheese Contest's "Havarti" category: Whole Milk Havarti

3rd place in 2018 World Championship Cheese Contest's "Washed Rind/Smear Ripened Hard Cheeses" category: Roth Grand Cru Reserve Wheel

1st place in 2018 World Championship Cheese Contest's "Pepper Flavored Cheeses, High Heat" category: Roth Chipotle Havarti Loaf

3rd place in 2018 World Championship Cheese Contest's "Latin American Style Hard Cheeses" category: Roth Original GranQueso Wheel

2nd place in 2018 World Championship Cheese Contest's "Open Class: Hard Cheeses" category: Roth Pavino Cheese Wheel

2nd place in 2018 World Championship Cheese Contest's "Open Class: Hard Cheeses with Natural Rind" category: Roth Grand Cru Reserve Block

Hook's Cheese Company

3rd place in 2017 American Cheese Society's Judging & Competition's "Rindless Blue-veined, Made from Mixed, or Other Milks" category: EWE CALF to be KIDding Blue

2nd place in 2017 American Cheese Society's Judging & Competition's "Rindless Blue-veined, Made from Sheep's Milk" category: Little Boy Blue

2nd place in in 2017 American Cheese Society's Judging & Competition's "Rindless Blue-veined, Made from Goat's Milk" category: Barneveld Blue

3rd place in 2017 American Cheese Society's Judging & Competition's "Rindless Blue-veined, Made from Cow's Milk" category: Traditional Blue

2nd place in 2017 American Cheese Society's Judging & Competition's "Open Category: American Made/International Style, Made from Sheep's Milk" category: Sheep Milk Butterkase

Landmark Creamery

3rd place in 2017 American Cheese Society's Judging & Competition's "Open Category: Washed Rind Cheeses Aged More Than 60 days, Up to 42% moisture, Made from Sheep's Milk" category: Anabasque

1st place in 2017 American Cheese Society's Judging & Competition's "Fresh Rindless Sheep's Milk Cheese Aged 0 to 30 Days" category: Petit Nuage

3rd place in 2017 American Cheese Society's Judging & Competition's "Sheep Cheese with Flavor Added, 100% Sheep's Milk" category: Savory Brebis

2nd place in 2017 American Cheese Society's Judging & Competition's "Sheep Cheese with Flavor Added, 100% Sheep's Milk" category: Everything Bagel Brebis

1st place in 2017 American Cheese Society's Judging & Competition's "Open Category: American Made/International Style, Made from Cow's Milk" category: Pecora Nocciola

1st place in 2017 US Championship Cheese Contest's "Soft & Semi-Soft Sheep's Milk Cheeses" category: Petit Nuage

Nordic Creamery

1st place in 2017 US Championship Cheese Contest's "Unsalted Butter" category: Cultured Butter

1st place in 2017 US Championship Cheese Contest's "Flavored Butter" category: Cinnamon/Sugar Butter

2nd place in 2017 US Championship Cheese Contest's "Flavored Butter" category: Garlic and Basil Butter

1st place in 2018 World Championship Cheese Contest's "Flavored Butter" category: Garlic and Basil Butter

Roelli Cheese

3rd place in 2017 American Cheese Society's Judging & Competition's "American Originals Original Recipe/Open Category, Made from Cow's Milk" category: Dunbarton

3rd place in 2017 US Championship Cheese Contest's "Bandaged Cheddar, Mild to Medium" category: Roelli Haus Select Mild

Southeast Wisconsin

Clock Shadow Creamery

2nd place in 2017 American Cheese Society's Judging & Competition's "Fresh Unripened Cheese with Flavor Added, All Milks" category: Quark with SA Braai Chutney

Northeast Wisconsin

BelGioioso Cheese

3rd place in 2017 American Cheese Society's Judging & Competition's "Rubbed-Rind Cheese with Added Flavor Ingredients Rubbed or Applied on the Exterior Surface of the Cheese Only, All Milks" category: La Bottega di Bel-Gioioso Artigiano Vino Rosso

1st place in 2017 American Cheese Society's Judging & Competition's "Rubbed-Rind Cheese with Added Flavor Ingredients Rubbed or Applied on the Exterior Surface of the Cheese Only, All Milks" category: La Bottega di Bel-Gioioso Artigiano Aged Balsamic & Cipolline Onion

2nd place in 2017 American Cheese Society's Judging & Competition's "Italian Type Cheeses: Grating Types (Aged Asiago, Domestic Parmesan, Grana, Reggianito, Sardo; Romano Made Only from Cow's or Goat's Milk), All Milks: Parmesan

1st place in 2017 American Cheese Society's Judging & Competition's "Mascarpone and Cream Cheese, Made from Cow's Milk" category: BelGioioso Crema di Mascarpone

3rd place in 2017 American Cheese Society's Judging & Competition's "Open Category, Fresh Unripened Cheeses, Cow's Milk" category: BelGioioso Crescenza-Stracchino

2nd place in 2017 US Championship Cheese Contest's "Natural Snack Cheese" category: BelGioioso Fresh Mozzarella Snacking Cheese

3rd place in 2017 US Championship Cheese Contest's "Soft & Semi-Soft Mixed Milk Cheeses" category: BelGioioso Crumbly Gorgonzola with Sheep's Milk

1st place in 2017 US Championship Cheese Contest's "Open Class: Flavored Soft Cheeses" category: BelGioioso Burrata with Black Truffles

3rd place in 2017 US Championship Cheese Contest's "Open Class: Flavored Soft Cheeses" category: Zesty Marinated Hand Braided Fresh Mozzarella

2nd place in 2017 US Championship Cheese Contest's "Ricotta" category: BelGioioso Ricotta con Latte Whole Milk

1st place in 2017 US Championship Cheese Contest's "Parmesan" category: BelGioioso Parmesan

2nd place in 2017 US Championship Cheese Contest's "Parmesan" category: American Grana

2nd place in 2017 US Championship Cheese Contest's "Fresh Asiago" category: BelGioioso Asiago

1st place in 2018 World Championship Cheese Contest's "Provolone, Aged" category: BelGioioso Aged Provolone Mandarini

1st place in 2018 World Championship Cheese Contest's "Parmesan" category: BelGioioso Parmesan

1st place in 2018 World Championship Cheese Contest's "Gorgonzola" category: BelGioioso CreamyGorg

1st place in 2018 World Championship Cheese Contest's "Open Class: Soft Cheeses" category: BelGioioso Mascarpone

2nd place in 2018 World Championship Cheese Contest's "Open Class: Soft Cheeses" category: BelGioioso Crema di Mascarpone

2nd place in 2018 World Championship Cheese Contest's "Open Class: Flavored Soft Cheeses" category: BelGioioso Burrata with Black Truffles

3rd place in 2018 World Championship Cheese Contest's "Soft & Semi-Soft (Semi-Hard) Mixed Milk Cheeses" category: BelGioioso Crumbly Gorgonzola with Sheep's Milk

1st place in 2018 World Championship Cheese Contest's "Natural Snack Cheese" category: BelGioioso Fresh Mozzarella Snacking Cheese

LaClare Family Creamery
3rd place in 2017 American Cheese Society's Judging & Competition's "Farmstead Category Aged 60 Days or More, Made from Goat's Milk" category: LaClare Farms Evalon

3rd place in 2017 American Cheese Society's Judging & Competition's "American Originals Original Recipe/Open Category, Made from Mixed or Other Milks" category: LaClare Farms Cave Aged Chandoka

3rd place in 2017 US Championship Cheese Contest's "Hard Goat's Milk Cheeses" category: Grevalon

2nd place in 2017 US Championship Cheese Contest's "Semi-Soft Goat's Milk Cheeses" category: Goat Milk Feta

2nd place in 2018 World Championship Cheese Contest's "Hard Mixed Milk Cheeses" category: Chandoka

1st place in 2018 World Championship Cheese Contest's "Surface (Mold) Ripened Mixed Milk Cheeses" category: Cave Aged Chandoka NZ Cheddar Style Mixed

Red Barn Family Farms
1st place in 2017 US Championship Cheese Contest's "Bandaged Cheddar, Sharp to Aged" category

2nd place in 2017 US Championship Cheese Contest's "Bandaged Cheddar, Mild to Medium" category

3rd place in 2018 World Championship Cheese Contest's "Traditional Waxed Cheddar, Mild to Medium" category: Heritage Weis Cheddar Cheese

1st place in 2018 World Championship Cheese Contest's "Traditional Waxed Cheddar, Sharp to Aged" category: Aged Cheddar

2nd place in 2018 World Championship Cheese Contest's "Traditional Waxed Cheddar, Sharp to Aged" category: Aged Heritage Weis Cheddar Cheese

3rd place in 2018 World Championship Cheese Contest's "Traditional Waxed Cheddar, Sharp to Aged" category: Aged Heritage Weis Cheddar Cheese

Renard's
1st place in 2017 American Cheese Society's Judging & Competition's "Reduced Fat Cheese with Flavor Added, All Milks" category: Pesto Farmers Cheese

3rd place in 2017 American Cheese Society's Judging & Competition's "Cheese Curds, All Milks" category: Cheddar Cheese Curds

Sartori
2017 US Champion in US Championship Cheese Contest: Reserve Black Pepper BellaVitano

3rd place in 2017 American Cheese Society's Judging & Competition's "Cheeses Marinated in Liquids and Ingredients, Made from Cow's Milk" category: Sartori Reserve Balsamic BellaVitano

3rd place in 2017 American Cheese Society's Judging & Competition's "Cheeses Marinated in Liquids and Ingredients, Made from Cow's Milk" category: Sartori Reserve Merlot BellaVitano

3rd place in 2017 American Cheese Society's Judging & Competition's "Goat's Milk Cheese Aged Over 60 Days" category: Sartori Limited Edition Extra-Aged Goat

3rd place in 2017 American Cheese Society's Judging & Competition's "Open Category: American Made/International Style, Made from Mixed, or Other Milks" category: Sartori Limited Edition Pastorale Blend

1st place in 2017 US Championship Cheese Contest's "Hard Mixed Milk Cheeses" category: Sartori Tre Donnes

2nd place in 2017 US Championship Cheese Contest's "Hard Mixed Milk Cheeses" category: Sartori Limited Edition Pastorale Blend

1st place in 2017 US Championship Cheese Contest's "Open Class: Flavored Hard Cheeses" category: Sartori Reserve Black Pepper BellaVitano

2nd place in 2017 US Championship Cheese Contest's "Open Class: Flavored Hard Cheeses" category: Sartori Reserve Citrus Ginger BellaVitano

3rd place in 2017 US Championship Cheese Contest's "Open Class: Flavored Hard Cheeses" category: Sartori Reserve Herbs de Provence BellaVitano

3rd place in 2017 US Championship Cheese Contest's "Open Class: Flavored Cheeses with Sweet Condiments" category: Sartori Reserve Rum Runner BellaVitano

2nd place in 2017 US Championship Cheese Contest's "Aged Asiago (Over 6 Months)" category: Sartori Reserve Extra-Aged Asiago

3rd place in 2017 US Championship Cheese Contest's "Aged Asiago (Over 6 Months)" category: Sartori Classic Asiago

1st place in 2018 World Championship Cheese Contest's "Hard Mixed Milk Cheeses" category: Sartori Limited Edition Pastorale Blend

2nd place in 2018 World Championship Cheese Contest's "Aged Asiago (Over 6 Months)" category: Sartori Reserve Extra-Aged Asiago

1st place in 2018 World Championship Cheese Contest's "Open Class: Flavored Cheeses with Sweet or 'Dessert' Condiments" category: Sartori Reserve Espresso BellaVitano

2nd place in 2018 World Championship Cheese Contest's "Open Class: Flavored Cheeses with Sweet or 'Dessert' Condiments" category: Sartori Reserve Merlot BellaVitano

2nd place in 2018 World Championship Cheese Contest's "Open Class: Flavored Hard Cheeses" category: Sartori Reserve Black Pepper BellaVitano

Saxon Creamery

3rd place in 2017 US Championship Cheese Contest's "Cold Pack Cheese Spreads" category: Gouda Cold Pack Cheese Spread

2nd place in 2017 US Championship Cheese Contest's "Open Class: Hard Cheeses" category: Alpine Style Aged 22 Months

3rd place in 2017 US Championship Cheese Contest's "Open Class: Hard Cheeses" category: Alpine Style Aged 12 Months

1st place in 2017 US Championship Cheese Contest's "Open Class: Pepper Flavored Cheese, Medium Heat" category: Gouda with Serrano Peppers Aged 9 Months

1st place in 2017 US Championship Cheese Contest's "Smoked Gouda" category: Smoked Gouda Aged 7 Months

2nd place in 2017 US Championship Cheese Contest's "Smoked Gouda" category: Smoked Gouda Aged 8 Months

3rd place in 2017 US Championship Cheese Contest's "Fresh Asiago" category: Whole Milk Asiago (Fresh Style) Aged 4 Months

1st place in 2017 US Championship Cheese Contest's "Bandaged Cheddar, Mild to Medium" category: Old English Style Cheddar Aged 5 Months

2nd place in 2018 World Championship Cheese Contest's "Traditional Waxed Cheddar, Mild to Medium" category: Old English Style Cheddar Aged 5 Months

1st place in 2018 World Championship Cheese Contest's "Fresh Asiago" category: Whole Milk Asiago (Fresh Style) Aged 5 Months

1st place in 2018 World Championship Cheese Contest's "Gouda, Mild" category: Gouda Aged 3 Months

1st place in 2018 World Championship Cheese Contest's "Smoked Gouda" category: Smoked Gouda Aged 8 Months

1st place in 2018 World Championship Cheese Contest's "Smoked Gouda" category: Smoked Gouda Aged 3 Months

3rd place in 2018 World Championship Cheese Contest's "Open Class: Hard Cheeses" category: Alpine Style Aged 16 Months

Widmer's Cheese Cellars
3rd place in 2017 American Cheese Society's Judging & Competition's "Brick Cheese, Made from Cow's Milk" category: Mild Brick Cheese

1st place in 2017 US Championship Cheese Contest's "Cold Pack Cheese, Cheese Food" category: Traditional Washed Rind Aged Brick Spread

Northwest Wisconsin

Burnett Dairy Cheese
3rd place in 2017 US Championship Cheese Contest's "Colby" category: Colby #1

Ellsworth Cooperative Creamery
3rd place in 2017 American Cheese Society's Judging & Competition's "Monterey Jack with Flavor Added, All Milks" category: Ghost Pepper Jack

2nd place in 2017 American Cheese Society's Judging & Competition's "Monterey Jack with Flavor Added, All Milks" category: Hot Pepper Jack

2nd place in 2017 American Cheese Society's Judging & Competition's "Brick Muenster, Made from Cow's Milk" category: Red Rind Muenster

Holland's Family Cheese
2017 Second Runner Up in 2018 US Championship Cheese Contest: Marieke Gouda Belegen

1st place in 2017 American Cheese Society's Judging & Competition's "Open Category: Smoked Cheeses, Made from Cow's Milk" category: Marieke Gouda Smoked

3rd place in 2017 American Cheese Society's Judging & Competition's "International-Style with Flavor Added, All Milks" category: Marieke Gouda Onion Garlic

3rd place in 2017 American Cheese Society's Judging & Competition's "Dutch-style, All Milks" category: Marieke Gouda Aged (9–12 months)

2nd place in 2017 US Championship Cheese Contest's "Open Class: Flavored Semi-Soft (Semi-Hard) Cheeses" category: Marieke Gouda Honey Clover

2nd and 3rd place in 2017 US Championship Cheese Contest's "Open Class: Semi-Soft Cheeses" category: Marieke Golden

3rd place in 2017 US Championship Cheese Contest's "Smoked Gouda" category: Marieke Gouda Smoked Cumin

1st place in 2017 US Championship Cheese Contest's "Edam & Gouda" category: Marieke Gouda Belegen

3rd place in 2017 US Championship Cheese Contest's "Edam & Gouda" category: Marieke Gouda Belegen (4–6 months)

1st and 2nd place in 2017 US Championship Cheese Contest's "Gouda, Aged" category: Marieke Gouda Aged

1st and 2nd place in 2017 US Championship Cheese Contest's "Gouda, Aged" category: Marieke Gouda Mature

2nd place in 2017 US Championship Cheese Contest's "Gouda, Flavored" category: Marieke Gouda Truffle

3rd place in 2017 US Championship Cheese Contest's "Gouda, Flavored" category: Marieke Gouda Bacon

2nd place in 2017 US Championship Cheese Contest's "Gouda, Aged" category: Marieke Gouda Aged

2nd place in 2018 World Championship Cheese Contest's "Gouda, Mild" category: Marieke Gouda Belegen (4–6 months)

3rd place in 2018 World Championship Cheese Contest's "Gouda, Mild" category: Marieke Gouda Young

1st place in 2018 World Championship Cheese Contest's "Gouda, Flavored" category: Marieke Gouda Onion Garlic

3rd place in 2018 World Championship Cheese Contest's "Gouda, Flavored" category: Marieke Gouda Cumin

3rd place in 2018 World Championship Cheese Contest's "Open Class: Flavored Cheeses with Sweet or 'Dessert' Condiments" category: Marieke Gouda Honeyclover

Yellow Door Creamery

3rd place in 2017 American Cheese Society's Judging & Competition's "Raclette-style: Aged over 45 Days, All Milks" category: Yellow Door Creamery Valis

2nd place in 2017 American Cheese Society's Judging & Competition's "Rubbed-Rind Cheese with Added Flavor Ingredients Rubbed or Applied on the Exterior Surface of the Cheese Only, All Milks" category: Yellow Door Creamery Tuscan Herb Rubbed Fontal

3rd place in 2017 American Cheese Society's Judging & Competition's "Open Category/American Made/International Style, Made from Cow's Milk" category: Yellow Door Creamery Monte

1st place in 2017 US Championship Cheese Contest's "Open Class: Flavored Semi-Soft (Semi-Hard) Cheeses" category: Yellow Door Creamery Harissa Rubbed Fontal Cheese

2nd place in 2018 World Championship Cheese Contest's "Open Class: Flavored Semi-Soft (Semi-Hard) Cheeses" category: Yellow Door Creamery Tuscan Rubbed Fontal Cheese

3rd place in 2018 World Championship Cheese Contest's "Open Class: Flavored Semi-Soft (Semi-Hard) Cheeses" category: Yellow Door Creamery Bergamot Hibiscus Rubbed Fontal

Appendix B
Annual Cheese Events

April

Late April: Wisconsin Grilled Cheese Championship, Dodgeville, grilledcheesewisconsin.com

Think you can make a mean grilled-cheese sandwich? You might want to enroll in this competition where judges range from the local mayor to cheesemakers, plus food bloggers and culinary instructors. Competitors are organized into amateur and professional levels, plus a Young Chefs category for budding foodies between the ages of twelve and seventeen. Four sandwich categories—Classic, Classic Plus One, Classic Plus Extras, and Dessert—ensure plenty of twists on the standard grilled-cheese 'wich. All contestants must use Wisconsin cheese in their recipes.

Late April: Between the Bluffs Beer, Wine & Cheese Festival, La Crosse, beerwinecheese.explorelacrosse.com

Admission price for this festival, which has been going strong since 2002 with cheese added in subsequent years, includes samples of cheese, beer, and wine plus a pint glass to keep. Upgrade to VIP tickets for a catered meal and access to specialty artisan cheeses from around Wisconsin. Cheese vendors are listed before the festival each year. Past years have included Capri Cheese, White Jasmine, and Hook's Cheese Company.

May

Late May: The Big Cheese Event at The Osthoff Resort in Elkhart Lake, thebigcheeseosthoff.com

This event was hosted for the first time in 2018, bringing together cheese lovers and experts in all things cheese (yes, there are tastings as well as a cheese marketplace, so bring your cooler!). Participating cheesemakers from the region include Sartori, LaClare Farms, Saxon Creamery, and Sargento. Attendees get the cheese treatment from head to toe at this luxury resort during The Big Cheese Event, from a cleansing milk spa treatment in the spa to a cheese and cocktail cruise around the lake, plus a nine-course dinner folding in artisan cheeses and a cheesemaking class in The Osthoff Resort's L'Ecole de la Maison cooking school.

Late May: Curds & Kegs at the West Allis Farmers Market, West Allis, westallisfarmersmarket.com/tag/curds-kegs

Locals know that West Allis has one of the Milwaukee area's best farmers' markets, held on Tuesdays, Thursdays and Saturdays between the first Saturday in May and Thanksgiving. It's also the site of Curds & Kegs, where—for the price of admission—eighty different cheeses can be sampled, paired with Wisconsin craft beer, of course. It's sponsored by West Allis Cheese & Sausage Shoppe, with locations in West Allis and the Milwaukee Public Market.

June

Early June: Beer, Bacon & Cheese Fest, New Glarus
As the name implies, this festival is all about drinking Wisconsin craft beer and enjoying what goes best with it: bacon and cheese. Often the festival sells out, as it did in 2018, so get your tickets well in advance.

Early June: Great Wisconsin Cheese Festival, Little Chute, littlechutewi.com/226/ Great-Wisconsin-Cheese-Festival
Kicking off National Dairy Month each year is this cheese festival, with a Big Cheese Parade, fireworks, a Cheddar Chase 1-mile walk or run, and cheese tastings. Participants get to watch a cheese carver do his magic, too. This festival has been going strong for about thirty years.

Late June: Cheese Curd Festival, Ellsworth, cheesecurdfestival.com
Dubbed the cheese-curd capital of Wisconsin by a former governor, the moniker lives on at the annual Cheese Curd Festival. Events include a 5K and 10K "cheese curd run" through the countryside, a cheese marketplace, chef demos, a contest to see which craft brewer comes up with the best cheese pairing, and—naturally—tastings (here's your chance to try hickory-bacon or cinnamon-sugar-dessert curds!).

September

Early September: Cheese-A-Palooza, Kenosha, wisconsinscheeseapalooza.com
Kenosha's lakefront is gorgeous, and this is the perfect opportunity to check it out if you love cheese. The festival takes place at 54th Street and 6th Avenue. Food vendors dish up items that include deep-fried cheese curds and grilled-cheese sandwiches—because it wouldn't be a cheese festival without those, right? Alice in Dairyland (an agriculture ambassador for the state crowned each year) makes a visit, and there are a variety of eating contests, from who can eat the most cheese pizza to who can eat the most maca-roni and cheese.

Mid-September: Green County Cheese Days, Monroe, cheesedays.com
Believe it or not, in 2019 Cheese Days celebrates its 102nd year, a testament to how deep the roots at this festival go. Events include food vendors—a mix of local chefs and food trucks—showing off the many ways you can prepare food with cheese, including meat-and-cheese skewers, deep-fried cheese curds, grilled-cheese sandwiches, and macaroni and cheese. A slice of leading makers in Wisconsin's dairy industry shines through at the Swiss Colony Cheese Days Parade, with cheesemakers marching. There's even a com-memorative pie plate produced each year in partnership with Red Wing Stoneware & Pottery. Each year a cheese ambassador, king and queen, prince and princess, and Miss Cheese are crowned, too.

October

1st Saturday in October: Cheese Fest, Shullsburg, experienceshullsburg.com
Held in downtown Shullsburg—with its historical, charming storefronts—this family-friendly event brings together cheesemakers and chefs, plus tons of small-town events like a breakfast hosted by the fire department, the library's annual book sale, and a "Test Your Cheese IQ" contest.

Late October: Kohler Food & Wine Experience, Kohler, kohlerathome.com/events
One of Wisconsin's longest-running wine festivals, bringing in wine makers from top wine-making regions as well as celebrity chefs from across the country, there is also a focus on Wisconsin cheese at this four-day event. Seminars (which are often sold out, so sign up early) with Wisconsin cheesemakers are an opportunity to learn more about the state's creamery history as well as sample a portfolio of cheese. A grand tasting of wine and cheese is the undisputed highlight.

Appendix C
Wisconsin Cheese Retailers and Creameries

True supporters of Wisconsin artisan cheese are the cheesemongers. From Door County to the Driftless Region, these charming shops—or cheese counters, if in a larger store—help spread the word about what's trending. They are also happy to make recommendations for pairing your favorite cheese with a wine, craft beer, or cocktail. Don't be afraid to chat them up: They could talk cheese all day long!

Southwest Wisconsin

Alp & Dell Cheese Store, 657 2nd St., Monroe, (608) 328-3355, alpanddellcheese.com

Baumgartner's Cheese Store & Tavern, 1023 16th Ave., Monroe, (608) 325-6157, baumgartnercheese.com

Ehlenbach's Cheese Chalet, 4879 County Rd. V, DeForest, (608) 846-4791, ehlenbachscheese.com

Fromagination, 12 S. Carroll St., Madison, (608) 255-2430, fromagination.com

Market Square Cheese, 1150 Wisconsin Dells Pkwy. S., Lake Delton, (608) 254-8388, marketsquarecheese.com

Mousehouse Cheesehaus, 4494 Lake Circle, Windsor, (608) 846-4455, mousehousecheese.com

People's Food Co-op, 315 5th Ave. S., La Crosse, (608) 784-5798, pfc.coop

Regent Market Co-op, 2136 Regent St., Madison, (608) 233-4329, regentmarketcoop.org

Whole Foods Market, 3313 University Ave., Madison, (608) 233-9566, wholefoodsmarket.com

Willy Street Co-op, 1221 Williamson St., Madison, (608) 251-6776; 2817 N. Sherman Ave., Madison, (608) 471-4422; 6825 University Ave., Middleton, (608) 284-7800; willystreet.coop

Southeast Wisconsin

Bobby Nelson's Cheese Shop, 2924 120th Ave., Kenosha, (262) 859-2232

The Cheese Box, 801 S. Wells St., Lake Geneva, (262) 248-3440, cheesebox.com

Clock Shadow Creamery, 138 W. Bruce St., (414) 273-9711, clockshadowcreamery.com

Glorioso's Italian Market, 1011 E. Brady St., Milwaukee, (414) 272-0540, gloriosos.com

Larry's Brown Deer Market, 8737 N. Deerwood Dr., Milwaukee, (414) 355-9650, larrysmarket.com

Mars Cheese Castle, 2800 W. Frontage Rd., Kenosha, (855) 352-6277, marscheese.com

Outpost Natural Foods Co-op, 7590 W. Mequon Rd., Mequon, (262) 242-0426; 100 E. Capitol Dr., Milwaukee, (414) 961-2597; 7000 W. State St., Wauwatosa, (414) 778-2012; 2826 S. Kinnickinnic Ave., Milwaukee, (414) 755-3202; outpost.coop

Tenuta's Deli, 3203 52nd St., Kenosha, (262) 657-9001

The Village Cheese Shop, 1430 Underwood Ave., Wauwatosa, (414) 488-2099, villagecheesetosa.com

West Allis Cheese & Sausage Shoppe, 400 N. Water St. (inside the Milwaukee Public Market), (414) 289-8333, wacheese-gifts.com

Whole Foods Market, 2305 N. Prospect Ave., Milwaukee, (414) 223-1500; 11100 W. Burleigh St., Wauwatosa, (414) 808-3600; wholefoodsmarket.com

Wisconsin Cheese Mart, 215 W. Highland Ave., Milwaukee, (414) 272-3544, wisconsincheesemart.com

Northeast Wisconsin

Door Artisan Cheese Company, 8103 Hwy. 42 N., Egg Harbor, (920) 868-1444, doorartisancheese.com

Field to Fork, 511 S. 8th St., Sheboygan, (920) 694-0322, fieldtoforkcafe.com

Seguin's House of Cheese, W. 1968 US 41, Marinette, (800) 338-7919, seguinscheese.com

Simon's Specialty Cheese, 2735 Freedom Rd., Appleton, (920) 788-6311, simonscheese.com

Vern's Cheese, 312 W. Main St., Chilton, (920) 849-7717, vernscheese.com

Vintage Elkhart Lake, 100 E. Rhine St., Elkhart Lake, (920) 876-4846, vintageelkhartlake.com

Wisconsin Cheese Masters, 4692 Rainbow Ridge Ct., Egg Harbor, (920) 868-4320, wisconsincheesemasters.com

Woodlake Market, at The Shops at Woodlake Kohler, 795 Woodlake Rd., Kohler, (920) 457-6570, americanclub resort.com/shopping/woodlake-market

Woodman's Market, 2400 Duck Creek Pkwy., Green Bay, (920) 499-1480, woodmans-food.com

Northwest Wisconsin

Humbird Cheese, 2010 Eaton Ave., Tomah, (888) 684-5353, humbirdcheese.com

Just Local Food Co-op, 1117 S. Farwell St., Eau Claire, (715) 552-3366, justlocalfood.coop

Woodman's Market, 2855 Woodman Ave., Altoona, (715) 598-7255, woodmans.com

Z's Cheese Haus, 11 5th Ave. N., Hurley, (715) 561-4500, zscheesehaushurley.com

Acknowledgments

This book would not be possible without the cheesemakers, who set aside time to talk about their family histories, their favorite cheeses, and their love for Wisconsin. At times I felt like a wide-eyed city person, marveling at cows out at pasture, day-old baby goats, and Amish buggies, and asking a ton of questions, but when I got back into my car I felt knit with the landscape. I moved to Wisconsin from Illinois many years ago. Writing this book made me feel like a true Wisconsinite. Thank you, Dairy State, for welcoming me in.

Katie, you've been a dream editor to work with. Thank you for suggesting this project. I hope I've done it justice.

Dairy Farmers of Wisconsin is the kind of organization every group of farmers across the country needs. While cheesemakers are out milking the cows and aging the cheese, these folks provide marketing and exposure. They were also helpful to me in providing images, resources, and information when I needed it.

Writing can be a lonely endeavor. Thank you to my writer friends—Carrie Bell, Lisa Kaiser, Michael Timm, Elke Sommers, Brooke McEwen, Jon Etter, Sheila Julson Thompson, Neill Kleven, Danielle Switalski, and Lauren Sieben—who answer texts and emails and let me know you also know this road. And for everyone who asked, "How's the book going?"—especially Jennifer Stearns—I owe you a big wedge of cheese.

Thank you, Tony, for your support and enthusiasm, with not only this book but all my writing projects. "I'm your biggest fan" is one of the kindest things anyone has ever said to me. For this one, you held down the fort while I slept in motels across the state while researching this book. And every writer needs a dog who lies behind your desk chair, his tufts of hair at risk of getting caught in the wheels should you get up, and keeps giving you the "Are you done yet?" look, reminding you there's more to life than working at a computer. Thank you, Roadie, for that constant reminder.

Photo Credits

Index